Leadership in Japanese House Churches

Leadership in Japanese House Churches

Simon Cozens

Copyright © 2010 Simon Cozens

Published in 2010 by Wide Margin,
90 Sandyleaze, Gloucester, GL2 0PX, UK
http://www.wide-margin.co.uk/

The right of Simon Cozens to be identified as the Author of this Work has been asserted by him in accordance with the Copyright, Designs and Patents Act 1988.

All rights reserved. No part of this publication may be reproduced, stored in a retrieval system, or transmitted in any form or by any means electronic, or mechanical, photocopying, recording or otherwise, without the prior permission of the publisher or a licence permitting restricted copying.

ISBN 978-0-9565943-6-5

Printed and bound in Great Britain by Lightning Source, Milton Keynes

Introduction

Whenever I give a talk or a presentation on the state of mission in Japan, I am often asked why, after a hundred and fifty years of Protestant evangelism, the church has not grown. Often those asking the questions will share with me their answers to that question: spiritual darkness, ancestor worship, Buddhism, lack of Biblical teaching. Sometimes I will give a stock answer; other times I will point out that if we knew, we would do something about it.

Privately, however, I have become more and more convinced that the inhibiting factor for the Japanese church is, in fact, the Japanese church. In particular, I have come to believe that ecclesiological and sociological aspects of Japanese church leadership mitigate against the involvement of the laity and have lead to passive congregations 'outsourcing' the work of Christianity to the trusted professional minister. Perhaps, I thought, if we could train authentically Christian, authentically Japanese leaders for our churches, then the Japanese church could flourish. I began studying and teaching leadership development for the Japanese church.

And yet as time went on and my experience with Japanese churches grew, I also came to the realisation that a hundred and fifty years of tinkering with the forms of church have not brought us any progress; given the deep-seated nature of the cultural and sociological implications of Japanese leadership, perhaps more radical surgery is needed: and indeed, if the clergy is the problem, why not remove the clergy?

While grappling with the issue of how to declericalise the Japanese church, I attended a seminar by Mitsuo Fukuda, whom I had read and cited as a missiologist but who, I had heard, had now practically abandoned missiological theorising and plunged himself into house church planting. At the seminar, I learnt of his Ten-Gai-Nai theological schema and the methods he uses for planting house churches. I adopted Ten-Gai-Nai methods within my established church ministry, and attempted a 'hybrid' church plant using house church principles as a daughter church from an established church[1].

The next year, in June 2008, Dr. Fukuda announced the first Japan House Church Conference, and a hundred house church practitioners and interested observers gathered in Osaka to share reflections and observations on the house church movement. Here I saw clearly the vitality and the participation that I longed to see in my churches. At the conference, and in his writing since, Dr. Fukuda stressed the importance of leadership development within house church movements. But what kind of leaders would a declericalised church require? And what would such leaders do? What, indeed, does it mean to a lead a church when the church emphasises its leaderless nature?

This present study of course aims to answer those questions; but it also charts my mental and spiritual exploration

---

[1] It failed...but that is the subject for another thesis.

of house churches—both their potentials and their limitations—in a search for a form of church and a form of leadership that is both authentically Christian and authentically Japanese. May God cause his churches—and his leaders—to grow authentically in Japanese soil.

Contents

Introduction   iv

1   **House churches and leaders**   1
    1.1   House churches as historical phenomenon   3
        1.1.1   New Testament church   4
        1.1.2   John Wesley's "classes and bands"   8
        1.1.3   The British House Church Movement   10
    1.2   House churches as current church planting strategy   14
    1.3   Trends, distinctives and theologies   17
        1.3.1   Elders, apostles and five-fold ministries   17
        1.3.2   "Simple" structures   19
        1.3.3   The rise of mentoring and coaching   22
    1.4   Current understandings of leadership   23
    1.5   The routinization of charisma   25
    1.6   Conclusions: What does leadership *mean*?   28

2 The house church in Japan — 31

- 2.1 History of house church involvement in Japan — 32
- 2.2 Estimating the scope of the house church — 34
- 2.3 Ecclesiological characteristics — 36
- 2.4 Survey of leadership understandings — 37
- 2.5 Conclusions — 40

3 Case study: Ten-Gai-Nai churches — 43

- 3.1 A sketch of the Ten-Gai-Nai schema — 44
- 3.2 Is Ten-Gai-Nai Japanese... and does it matter? — 48
- 3.3 Ten-Gai-Nai leadership development — 51
- 3.4 What is leadership in Ten-Gai-Nai churches? — 54
- 3.5 Conclusions — 56

4 Functions of Japanese leadership — 57

- 4.1 The group model — 58
- 4.2 Diffuse leadership and trust relations — 59
- 4.3 Sociology of voluntary organisations — 63
- 4.4 Leadership theory — 69
- 4.5 Areas of omission and future work — 73
- 4.6 Evaluation — 74

5	Conclusion		75
	5.1	Fit with Japanese leadership functions	77
	5.2	Fit with ecclesiological self-understanding	78
	5.3	Applicability to wider church community	79
	5.4	Critiques and improvements	82
	5.5	Areas for future study	84

Bibliography 87

A	Survey questionnaire		101
B	Ten-Gai-Nai Cheat Sheet		105
C	Interviews		107
	C.1	Initial interview with M - 2009-10-01	107
	C.2	Initial interview with G - 2009-10-29	108
D	Church multiplication		111
	D.1	Interactivity and Every Member Ministry	127
	D.2	Leadership is catalysis	131
	D.3	Training disciples to evangelise	135
	D.4	Bringing 'have-not' churches back to life	139

Index of Citations 145

Chapter 1

The house churches and their leaders: an outline sketch

In this book, we shall be investigating the nature of leadership within the house church, and examining the objectives and goals of leadership within those churches. Indeed, for a movement that prides itself on having no 'leaders in the technical sense,' (Simson, 2001:94) we will consider to what degree leadership is necessary, and what form it takes.

The locus of our investigation will be Japan, and, as well as examining in detail one particular stream of the Japanese house church, we will survey the current state of the house church in Japan and its self-understanding of the nature of leadership.

However, we shall also be aware that the Japanese house church is a particular cultural expression of a global idea, and

CHAPTER 1. HOUSE CHURCHES AND LEADERS

so to answer these questions, we must begin at the global level: we will first examine the cultural history of house churches and their beliefs and practices. We will then focus on the expressions of house church currently existing in Japan, before clarifying the leadership philosophy and theology of these churches; we will examine the Ten-Gai-Nai stream of churches lead by Mitsuo Fukuda, as one of the most clearly enunciated examples of a Japanese house church leadership development programme; and then we shall consider the concept of leadership more generally in Japanese society, in order to determine whether the house church's leadership is a good 'fit' in its cultural milieu.

As we begin by observing the global house church movement, we are immediately faced with two problems. The first is a problem of terminology and definition: what is a house church? Both Walker (1998) and Turner (1989) had problems with the terminology, finding it too diverse. Our investigation will later show that as well as 'house church' referring to a wide variety of expressions of church, a similarly wide variety of different metaphors and labels of church practice—house church, simple church, organic church, Church Planting Movement, and so on—refer to essentially the same concept. For simplicity, we will call them all 'house church' except where distinction is necessary[1], and rather than starting from a working definition, we will examine models and examples and deduce a definition from our findings.

The second problem is one of documentation. Turner (1989) cites Hollenweger's argument that house churches represent a pre-literary, oral culture, and as a charismatic

---

[1] For brevity, we will refer to churches not displaying house church characteristics as 'gathered churches.'

movement, churches spend comparatively little time in writing either their own histories or detailed accounts of their doctrines. Further, academic studies of the house churches are thin on the ground, and therefore what literature we do possess is promotional and polemic rather than critical and analytical. Our study of house church leadership will therefore require some broader analytical treament of the house church phenomenon.

1.1 House churches as historical phenomenon

No proponent of house church methods would claim that what they are doing is something new; like many other movements throughout church history—both orthodox, such as the Methodists, and somewhat less orthodox, such as the Jehovah's Witnesses—current house church writers such as Simson (2001), Zdero (2007c), Viola (2008) and Cole (1999) see themselves in the mould of a restorationist movement attempting to recover the original essence of the New Testament.

The word 'restorationist' in connection with house churches should remind those British churchgoers of a certain age of one such movement, and there is much similarity between the 1970s Restorationist movement and its thought and the present generation of house church writers; Restorationism will give us a useful interpretative matrix through which to view the current sources. We will examine the history of the capital-R Restorationist movement shortly, but first let us consider the nature of the New Testament church, to ascertain whether the picture painted by the house church writers is an accurate one.

CHAPTER 1. HOUSE CHURCHES AND LEADERS

1.1.1 New Testament church

As with any restoration movement, the church of the book of Acts is held up as the model church *par excellence*: Simson (2001:7) speaks of 'building according to fundamental New Testament patterns'; Zdero (2007c:7) to bringing back 'New Testament-style Christianity to the earth'; Krupp and Woodrum (2007b) traces the 'Fall and Rise of the Church' away from, and back to, 'the pattern, power, and purposes of the church as revealed in the New Testament.' And, we are told, 'the first pattern for church, for a community of believers in Jesus Christ, was that of meeting in small groups in homes.' (Barnett, 2007)

Yet all of the subsequent descriptions of New Testament ecclesiology refer to very particular situations within the church: small group meetings from after, say, the stoning of Stephen of 35 A.D., after which we are told 'the Jerusalem Temple was declared out of bounds' (Simson, 2001:24) to Christians, [2] up until the time that house churches were 'derailed': either by gradual decline until total ruin at around 600 A.D., (Restorationist thought cited by Walker 1998) or by the Constantinian adoption of Christianity as state religion in 312 A.D. (Simson; Krupp and Woodrum; Zdero 2007b) or even by the clericalising of Clement in 95 A.D.! (Job, 2007)

The New Testament certainly does refer to meetings in houses, to meetings where congregants participate in the exercise of diverse charisms, (1 Co. 14:26ff.) to letters written to city churches without named leaders, and so on. But one wonders if the picture painted by house church advocates is in fact the *whole* picture.

[2] Yet see Acts 21:26.

1.1. House churches as historical phenomenon

First, Tiplady (2003:100) suggests that meeting in houses under a family structure is not something intrinsic to the nature of the church, but rather that 'the earliest Christians simply organized themselves according to the patterns available to them in wider society.' Tiplady further comments on the nature and structures of the developing church, and of modern mission agencies, as a 'borrowing' from prevailing cultural patterns, and suggests that if there *is* an intrinsic principle of Christian organisation, it is the conscious aping of the secular.

Second, the virulent anti-clericalism, and in particular the attack on the cultic patterns expressed in 1st Clement, show clearly the replacement theology of house church narrators. Sadly, despite the contributions of e.g. Sanders (1983) and the New Perspective school in stressing the Jewishness both of Paul's writing and the Early Church, situations of early Christian Temple service (Acts 3, 5, and, in particular, 21) are silently discarded; being 'very close to the Old Testament' (Simson, 2001:7) is seen negatively, as if a predominantly Jewish community would entirely displace their styles of worship and meeting overnight—they would not, as 1st Clement, Hebrews and particularly James demonstrate. Indeed, James' (2:2-3) directions for seating "in your synagogues" (εἰς συναγωγὴν ὑμῶν) do not fit the house church narrative in any way, nor does the discovery of the 3rd Century church at Dura-Europos, whose "evidently open and tolerated presence in the middle of a major Roman garrison town reveals that the history of the early Church was not simply a story of pagan persecution." (James, 2000)

Seeing the current house churches as a restoration movement with respect to the New Testament church unfortunately

CHAPTER 1. HOUSE CHURCHES AND LEADERS

loses sight of the New Testament church as a renewal movement with respect to Judaism. Further, in a highly selective reading of the available evidence we have of the nature of the early Church, any form of clericalisation, of structure and discipline in churches, whether it be Clement or the Didache or any other extra-Biblical church history, is interpreted as the deviation from the norm, as error. Once the narrative is established, all evidence of *formalisation* which does not fit the narrative is explained away as evidence of *decline*.

We will therefore take seriously the possibility that the understanding of church history related by house church restorationists is an idealized construct, reading back their current experiences into the ancient texts; this is made the more probable by the proponents' insistence that despite abortive attempts through time to restore what was so utterly fallen, we are indeed blessed to be alive now in the 21st century when the full restoration of the New Testament church is finally at hand!

What then of leadership within the early church? Feddes (2008) argues that the predominant model of the early church was as a household, but not in the way that house church proponents suggest: the Roman household formed part of a "larger network of relations" beyond the immediate family centered around the patronage of the householder, including up to a hundred people; in its cultural context, the "front part of the house" was a semi-public, rather than private, space. However, he also notes carefully that the church was not homogenous, and that Jewish households did not always follow the Greco-Roman *paterfamilias* system. Within the early churches, wives, children and slaves alike operated

1.1. House churches as historical phenomenon

leadership functions by exerting social influence upon the group. Feddes therefore uses the overarching motif of "caring for the household" as the duty and function of the New Testament leader.

White (1987) similarly considers the social role of the *paterfamilias* as patron and the practice of hospitality to be key to the legitimacy of Christian leaders in the early church; he argues (p. 225) that the "function of upbuilding" exercised by house church leaders is expressed in terms of maintaining patronal relationships: leadership is a spiritual gift, legitimized by ethical and social authority, characterised by service, love, and giving and receiving patronage.

Finally, Bulley (2000) uses primary documents to trace the routinization of charisma in the early church; his thesis is that while leadership was initially a function of gifting and charismatic authority, it was quickly replaced by the authority of office, and then even by the time of the Didache, "ministry, especially that in the churches' meetings, is mainly, in some cases solely, the responsibility of those recognised as leaders." (p. 234) Neither the patron model of leadership nor the Jewish cultic model make an appearance in Bulley's account of the first century church, but his study deals with the purely historical, rather than the socio-historical.

Combining these insights, we can draw a few conclusions about leadership within the early church. First, Feddes' model is useful in two areas: it shows that leadership was, and is, exercised both through recognised leaders (patrons of houses) and unrecognised leaders. In particular, the social influence of all members, especially those normally regarded as powerless, was a distinctive characteristic of Christian relationships. White tells us more about the function of a

CHAPTER 1. HOUSE CHURCHES AND LEADERS

leader: that the role of early church leaders was primarily to ensure the smooth conduct of relationships within the body of Christ, and to be a father figure to the family of God. One can easily see, then, how such a paternal understanding of leadership can become institutionalized, as Bulley claims, until a ministerial understanding of leadership became concentrated upon particular anointed individuals.

1.1.2 John Wesley's "classes and bands"

In the middle of the eighteenth century, John Wesley began to gather together friends, followers and believers into 'Societies', modelled (*qua* Tiplady, 2003:100) on the friendly societies usually formed at the time to provide mutual support in the areas of financial and social services. However, as the teaching of Wesley spread into revival, these Societies soon became too large for personal oversight and accountability, and the lack of adequate spiritual supervision meant that members became lax in their spiritual walk. (Wesley, 1860b:252, II.1)

At the same time, the Societies were purchasing their own buildings and raising funds by subscription, through the friendly society system. (*ibid.*, II.3) The subscriptions were organised into "classes" of twelve, with class leaders taking on responsibilities for those members who could not afford the subscriptions. The classes also formed a means for visiting each Society member on a regular basis in their houses to check their spiritual health. Wesley soon realised, however, that one-on-one visitation took up the class leaders' time and that often class members in service or in shared accomodation could not speak freely with their leaders during a meeting, and so the decision was made for classes to meet together one a week.

1.1. House churches as historical phenomenon

As these classes developed, members found themselves either struggling with "temptations of such a kind, as they knew not how to speak in a class," (*ibid.*, p.258:VI.1) or looking for exclusively Christian fellowship—as opposed to classes which were open to Society members who did not profess faith—and so formed smaller 'bands,' for the confession of sin and for prayer and worship. Bands were to meet together once a quarter for a 'love-feast' celebration.

From the writings we have quoted, it may seem as though bands and classes evolved organically in reponse to needs within the Society, yet it is interesting to note that in 1738 Wesley spent time with Zinzendorf and the Moravian brethren at Herrnhut, during which time he 'studied carefully the offices of the church and how the people were divided (especially their classes and bands).' (Wesley, 1860a:p120) This surely refers to the choir and band system described by Bovet and Seed (1896:48):

> These bands were always composed of persons of the same sex, and according to their different degrees of spiritual development... The influence of these bands was immense. Without them, Zinzendorf often declared, Herrnhut would never have become what it was. A still more important institution was that of "choirs." In these larger groups, the members were arranged according to age, and sex, and civic status... In each of these classes, certain members, designated "workers," were charged with a sort of ministry.

CHAPTER 1. HOUSE CHURCHES AND LEADERS

One may reasonably conclude, then, that Wesley appropriated the structures of Moravian spirituality in order to respond to needs emerging within the Methodist Societies.

It is important to note, when considering the claims of house church proponents who would associate themselves in the stream of church renewal that includes Wesleyan Methodism, that Wesley did not consider classes and bands to be sufficient for Christian growth by themselves; on the contrary, he was "still convinced that the only lasting arena for perfection is the Society", (Wesley, 1860a:298) groups of "several hundred."

Indeed, the class system was created as much for the purchase of buildings through mutual subscription—something anathematic to house church advocates—as for mutual accountability. Bands, likewise, arose administratively as a subdivision of a subdivision, rather than a spontaneous organic group. Hence, one should be be rather suspicious of claims, such as Krupp and Woodrum's (2007a:217), that 'church was seen in essence not as an organization'. Wesley was nothing if not organisational.

1.1.3 The British House Church Movement

Chapter 36 of Zdero (2007c) is entitled 'Case Study (Britain): A retrospective of the British House Church Movement of the 1970s', and reflects the influence of the Restorationist movement on current house church thinking.

We will consider this group of house churches for a variety of reasons: first, and most obviously, because house church proponents today claim a historical and spiritual continuity

1.1. House churches as historical phenomenon

with that movement; second, because several aspects of their theology and praxis, most notably their ecclesiology of apostles and the five-fold ministries, either have influenced or directly mirror the contemporary understandings of house church both globally and in the case of Japan; third, because the historical development of the understanding of leadership within these churches demonstrates a possible trajectory for house church movements in other countries. We also have the benefits of both historical distance and documentary evidence, both of which are lacking in more modern movements. (In terms of documentary evidence, Walker 1998 is magisterial, and Wright 1991 is a useful supplementary.)

The British House Church Movement was started in Devon in 1958, at conferences organized by former Brethren charismatic leaders, and in particular Arthur Wallis, and grew to include a number of independent church planters throughout the country. It was, as Turner (1989:90) has it, "the product of firing Brethren and Pentecostalist leadership in the crucible of the charismatic renewal," which although it may sound a confusing and contradictory mix, sums up well the movement's leadership self-understanding: the charismatic emphasis on directive power, the Brethren's anti-clericalism and the Baptist's democracy are all in evidence, at the same time.

Although emphatically (even today) a non-denominational movement in their own terms, the 'house churches'— which never *really* met in houses; more often they would meet in rented halls or borrowed church buildings—began not just gathering in numbers but also in structure. Small groups began to cluster together into larger meetings, and those initial church planters began to take a more formal networking role.

CHAPTER 1. HOUSE CHURCHES AND LEADERS

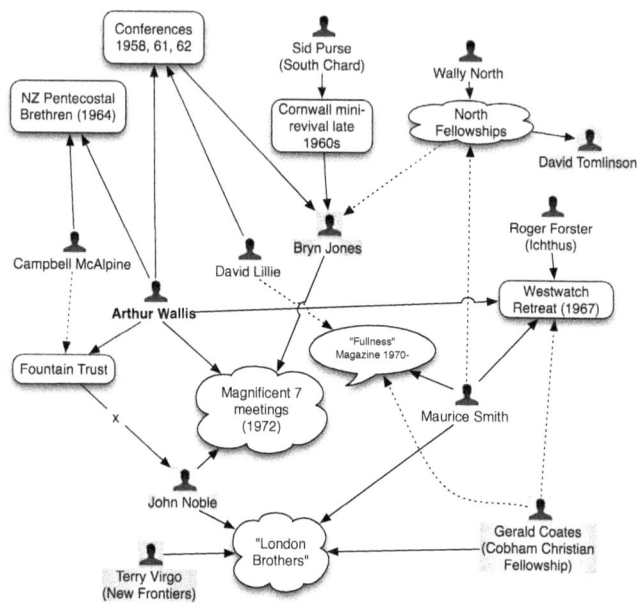

Figure 1.1: Schematic History of Restorationism, including key figures

While still preaching the evils of denominationism, the 'house churches' bought large buildings, established Bible colleges and schools, and adopted a leadership structure, as we shall see later, based around Ephesians 4. Eventually, as both Walker (2002) and Wright (1991) describe it, they became indistinguishable from the denominations from which they sought to break.

Walker (1998:173) sums up this paradox well:

1.1. House churches as historical phenomenon

Restorationism, by adopting the ecclesiology of Ephesians chapter 4, adopts with it an organizational pattern. To put it this way is not to present it as Restorationists would do themselves. They would say that to accept God's theocracy is to enter into a series of covenanted relationships with those leaders that God has ordained should rule in his Church.

One area in which these 'covenanted relationships' impact upon the praxis of the church is the emphasis on discipling, and in particular on direct accountability relationships. The nascent house churches were criticized from within and without for authoritarian tendencies in discipling, so-called 'heavy shepherding' (Walker, 1998:288ff.) and this gives us an insight into the understanding of leadership within these churches. The 'organizational pattern' of which Walker speaks was, primarily, a hierarchical, pyramid structure—apostles supervised pastors, pastors supervised elders, elders supervised cell group leaders and they supervised those in their group. Structurally this much is not dissimilar to gathered church structures, but Turner (1989:87) notes that "the (sociologically) radical character of its discipleship, that is, its comprehensive social control by leaders, and the unusual strength of personal commitment by members" set Restorationism's ecclesiology apart from the rest of the church.

Leadership in these churches, therefore, is delegated, covenanted and primarily pastoral.

1.2 House churches as current church planting strategy

Attempting to understand the resurgence of interest in the house churches in the US during the 1970s, Reid (1980) evaluates whether or not such a model could be viable for Southern Baptist Convention ministry. Reid's conclusions were published in *Home Mission*, the journal of the SBC's Home Missions Board. While some house churches developed within the SBC in the US, house church planting was not adopted as a deliberate strategy.

In 1998, however, the International Missions Board of the Southern Baptist Convention, the fifth-largest missionary sending organisation (Johnstone et al., 2001), announced a new vision statement reflecting a key strategy change:

> We will facilitate the lost coming to saving faith in Jesus Christ by beginning and nurturing Church Planting Movements among all peoples. (Garrison, 1999:7)

Garrison further defines a Church Planting Movement (hereafter "CPM") as "a rapid and multiplicative increase of indigenous churches planting churches within a given people group or population segment." (*ibid.*) To achieve rapid multiplication, changes were required the structural understanding of the nature of church: missionary involvement should be catalytical rather than ongoing; church growth should involve congregational multiplication rather than agglutination; leaders needed to be indigenous, bivocational laity rather than professional clergy; leadership training was to be on-the-job and mentoring-based rather than a time-consuming seminary course outside of the ministry setting. In other words, 5,000 missionaries found themselves suddenly committed to establishing house churches all over the world—in some cases, against their better judgment!

Despite the grass-roots, lay-led nature of these movements, Garrison (2010) claims that "leaders are so indispensable to Church Planting Movements" and suggests a variety of options to form a leadership development process. There is no discussion of the nature and role of leadership, but leaders are qualified as having

> manageable sized tasks (i.e. house churches as opposed to mega-churches), mutually accountable co-laborers (as opposed to stand alone leaders), and self-feeding capabilities (as opposed to dependency on outsiders for answers).

In short, it seems from this and some of the suggested development processes ("missionaries have supplemented other leadership development efforts by importing Pastor Study Bibles that are practically seminaries-in-a-book") that the CPM understanding of a leader is of a fairly traditional pastoral role, exercised within the small context of a house church, backed up by a hierarchical chain of leaders. ("one India movement cascaded leadership training from a leader to about 20 trainers who then trained a dozen pastors")

Further, despite assertions by Garrison (2004) that the CPM strategy was formed by a recognition of, and distillation of principles from, spontaneous church multiplications reported independently by IMB missionaries, Fowlkes

(2004:43) points out strong parallels with McGavran and Wagner (1990)'s theory of 'people movements', leading him to conclude that "the International Mission Board is embracing the strategy/model that was proposed and expounded by Donald McGavran approximately forty-five years earlier."

Even if Garrison's story of learning from historical spontaneous church multiplications is accurate, however, attempting to replicate these multiplications mechanistically by the adduction of principles brings to mind Wright's (2003:127) distinction between revival (the claimed spontaneous multiplications) and revivalism; (the principles thus adduced) unfortunately, the evidence is simply not yet available as to whether Wright's maxim that 'revival quickens, revivalism deadens' will apply in this case.

On this point a note of caution must be sounded: despite the commitment to the house church model espoused by the IMB, the consequent glut of theses and articles (to which Fowlkes himself is a contributor) developing a CPM strategy for this people or that people, and the obvious impact of 5,000 dedicated church planters around the world, we find no empirical studies, no follow-up surveys, no critical analyses of the lasting implications of CPM house churches. The strategy has been decided, but the evaluation is not yet done.

As we have seen with the house church movement in general, writers on CPM, such as Garrison (1999), are generally writing as proponents to persuade rather than analysts to document, and leave us no evidence—and plenty of counterevidence—that CPM will not go the way of the Methodists, the British house churches and, indeed, the Early Church itself.

Nevertheless, the commitment of IMB and other missions to CPM, and its favour amongst missionary practitioners, suggest that the house church phenomenon is again set to become a matter for timely investigation amongst missiologists and mission strategists.

1.3 Trends, distinctives and theologies

From the point of view of understanding leadership within the house churches, there are a number of distinct trends which have come together over the years to create the current picture of house church, and which exert their influence on the structures and leadership praxis of the house church, both globally and especially for our purposes, in Japan.

Our working understanding of house church, then, will be the set of ecclesial patterns formed by the fusion of these three strands: the five-fold ministries concept, the push for "simple" church, and the rise of mentoring and coaching.

1.3.1 Elders, apostles and five-fold ministries

One interesting distinctive of house churches which is significant for the purposes of our research is what practitioners would describe as the rediscovery of the 'five-fold ministries': drawing on Ephesians 4:11-12, a key part of both Restorationist ecclesiology and the ecclesiology of modern house church proponents is the re-establishment of anointed apostles, prophets, evangelists, pastors and teachers within the body of fellowship.

CHAPTER 1. HOUSE CHURCHES AND LEADERS

While most churches acknowledge almost all of these roles, the role of apostle is not generally acknowledged to be still valid. One of the central claims of Restorationist ecclesiology is that the apostolic role is not merely *valid* for today but is an *essential* part of church structure. Turner (1989:95) writes that the 'precise origins of this belief is unclear,' but in a footnote gives Watchman Nee's 'The Normal Christian Church Life' as a proximate source.

Turner also notes (p. 103) that the chains of authority in Restorationist churches have gradually weakened and the role of the apostle has become less directive and more advisory, but in the US, where the apostolic concept has been popularised by Wagner (1998b) and rebranded as the 'New Apostolic Reformation,' the reverse appears to have happened. Given Wagner's influence within the Church Growth Movement, it is not unreasonable to conclude that the recent resurgence of interest in apostolic churches, particularly in the US, (Miller, 1999:19) is a result of his intervention into the area. That house churches have picked up and centralised the concept of an apostolic restoration can be seen from such writers as Simson (2007), Zdero (2007a) and, from the point of view of the Japanese house church specifically, chapter 16 of Fukuda 2010.

For our purposes, one interesting dynamic of the house churches' understanding of apostles is that idea that apostles are not trained or ordained, but recognised: an apostle is anyone who behaves like an apostle. (Turner, 1989:92) Turner goes on to say (p. 97) that the role of an apostle involves

> (1) promoting the internal unity and rise to maturity of individual congregations (by the

> teaching, example and discipline exerted by the leaders under their leadership), (2) providing the visible unity between dependent congregations ... and (3) providing the link between different apostolic works ... thus potentially providing the focus, or cement, of unity for the whole church.

We will return to this definition later, as it provides an incredibly useful bridge to the Japanese cultural environment.

Leadership in this context is expressed through a chain of such one-to-one accountability relationships (Turner, 1989:102ff.) seen as instituted by God and headed by the apostles; however, leadership is expressed within the context of a charismatic body whose prophetic functions include, at least in theory, challenging and correcting the abuses of leadership. Turner, as an emic commentator from within a Restorationist church, asserts that the authoritative nature of submission leadership is always perfectly counterbalanced by the prophetic function of the body, but given that the apostles and church leaders have titular authority in a way that prophets do not—the office of prophet is not, as it were, on the church's organisational chart—there are no safeguards against prophets being overruled, and indeed Wagner's allies such as Eckhardt (1999:25) state explicitly that *all* church offices need to be "willing to submit our ministry to a specific Apostolic visionary"—something, the cynic might remark, which is easy for a self-proclaimed apostolic visionary to declare. The will to power dies hard.

1.3.2 "Simple" structures

Parallel to the rise of apostolic thinking in Restorationist-style churches both in the UK and in the US has been the championing of church styles that remove or limit hierarchical structures. Known variously as "natural" church and "simple" church (See Dale and Dale, 2002; Viola, 2008) these normally take organic metaphors as a basis for ecclesiology—Cole (1999), for instance, speaks of "cultivating" a life for God. Church Planting Movements sits to some degree within this trend, in attempting to find agile methods for rapid church growth by stripping away many of the trappings of gathered church, but there is an important distinction: whereas CPM maintains the role of the pastor as primary teacher, the simple church movements emphasise peer-to-peer learning and de-emphasise the role of a full-time ordained pastor as positional leader.

These movements have not yet been studied academically, but through various shared concepts, not least the organic metaphor, I would surmise that they find a common ancestor in Schwarz's (1996) "Natural Church Development", which was written to correct some of the more mechanistic tendencies in the Church Growth Movement. One may go back further to the *comunidades eclesiales de base* of the late 1960s (Boff, 1986) to see examples of the shift that was noted and predicted by Bosch (1991:467):

> The movement away from ministry as the monopoly of ordained men to ministry as the responsibility of the whole people of God, ordained as well as non-ordained, is one of the most dramatic shifts taking place in the church today.

However, these movements are surely also part of a more widespread tendency in the society of the late 20th and

1.3. Trends, distinctives and theologies

early 21st centuries; Brafman and Beckstrom (2006) chart how "de-hierarchicalization" is a common conceit at present. Indeed, it is only natural, as it were, that the postmodern generation with its mistrust of authority figures should be searching for a new model of church that is based around the horizontal relationships of peer groups. While Wagner may be claiming that his apostolic network is the firstfruits of the second Reformation, (Wagner, 1998a) it is postmodernity that is actually driving sections of the church to remove the intermediaries between God and man.

What does it mean for leadership when churches center around distinct groups of peers? In a sense, this is the entire focus of this paper. But Brafman and Beckstrom (2006:109ff.) provide some hints. In their understanding of "leaderless organisations," there is still the distinct role of the *catalyst*, someone who radiates optimism, trust and empowerment without necessarily holding any formal power themselves. The catalyst has a role in connecting people between distinct networks and then, like their chemical equivalents, remaining separate to the reaction that then takes place, meaning that at bottom, "everyone is in charge of the movement's success, and everyone is an equal participant." (p. 209) So it is in the house churches—just like the apostles in more centralized contexts, whose role is "promoting the internal unity and rise to maturity of individual congregations ... and providing the link between different apostolic works," house church leaders are the social glue which provides the environment for every member to play their own part in ministry.

1.3.3 The rise of mentoring and coaching

Coaching is a subject that has come into vogue in the past fifteen years. The ATLA database of theological articles records 148 journal articles with the word "coaching" or "mentoring" in the title, and we will use the publication of missiological articles as a proxy measure of the popularity of the phenomenon. The earliest article dates from 1983, and there were five articles in the decade from 1980 to 1989; between 1990 and 1994, there were 16; between 1995 and 1999, there were 33. 2000 to 2004 saw the peak of the mentoring phenomenon with 62 articles published.

As large churches, particularly in the US, adopted more of a corporate metaphor for their activities, with the pastor as CEO of a business, (Morgenthaler, 2007:180–181) they introduced innovations from the business world into their leadership praxis. Corporate accountability culture has brought continuous professional development and staff appraisals into the ecclesiastical workplace; at the same time, the nature of leadership changed in the secular world to include emphasis on issues of character and integrity, and integrated reflective practices from the American culture of therapy and self-help. (Goleman et al., 2003)

Executive coaching became the *de facto* way of leadership development in the corporate sector, (Thach, 2002) and from there came into the church. For the house churches, it provides a relational, semi-structured method of teaching that fits well with the accountability structures already in place.

These three factors—five-fold and apostolic ministries, simple structures, and coaching and mentoring—make up the ecclesiological distinctives of the house church phenomenon.

1.4 Current understandings of leadership

We have already noted Simson's claim that house churches have 'no leaders in the technical sense.' Zdero (2007c) is a collection of articles on the house churches, and contains the following sentences about house church leadership: (emphasis mine)

- "[House church] is the experience of being in a face-to-face community with Jesus Christ as the *group's only head*."

- "Participation will come from *everyone* as they learn to function as members of Christ's Body. Leadership will come from the Holy Spirit through the Body."

- "These households of faith are typically *led locally by elders* and networked together by the *five-fold ministries*. David Bennett has observed *five types of leadership*, each with differing roles in God's unfolding plan in the current house church movement of India." [These level types are the man of peace, the believer, the disciple, the elders, the five-fold ministers.]

- "Any distinction between elder, presbyter, overseer, pastor and shepherd by the creation of a formal, local, *leader-over-leader hierarchy would have done against the apostolic pattern*. Thus, *elders*, by far the most common term used for local church leaders, *were the primary faciliators* of household churches in the first century."

CHAPTER 1. HOUSE CHURCHES AND LEADERS

- "The *top leaders* asked their *provincial and regional leaders* to submit reports. These people then gathered the statistics from *grassroots house church leaders*, who operated at the city and county level."

- "If we have multiplying house churches, which create an exponential growth rate, we need a leadership development structure which grows as fast as the churches multiply. This chapter explores the role of the five-fold ministries of *apostles, prophets, evangelists, pastors and teachers* for multiplying house church networks."

- "However, trust and teamwork between *local and translocal leaders* needs to be nurtured to ensure this is *not done in a hierarchical way*."

We can therefore presume that there is a plurality of opinions as to the nature and offices of house church leadership—or rather, that the house church holds in tension the opposing tendencies of hierarchical apostolic leadership and simple peer leadership. How house proponents manage to hold this tension without slipping into cognitive dissonance is a matter of opinion; my belief is that there is a confusion even in their minds about what they understand leadership to be.

A slip of the pen in early draft of the proposal for this research ended up referring to 'flat hierarchies' within the house churches—I was challenged as to whether I meant flat structures or hierarchical structures, since one obviously cannot have both. But I have become convinced that the phrase 'flat hierarchies' ideally reflects the contradiction inherent in house churches today between the peer-to-peer model of the simple church and the hierarchical model of the apostolic church.

To understand this we must separate the functions contained within our understanding of a church leader: there are organizational, social, educational, pastoral and liturgal functions, to name but a few. House churches seem to reserve some of these functions to the groups themselves as corporate entities and some to leader figures as distinct individuals. Organizationally, the leader has a role in networking together disparate house church groups. The social and liturgical function of the house church leader inside the community is one of cohesion and order—the *facilitador* of the base ecclesial communities; educationally, however, the church leader is placed within the community as a teacher amongst peer teachers, albeit perhaps as one prized for their maturity and the teaching they have received from others rather than for their positional authority. Pastorally, everyone leads everyone else, both corporately in peer-to-peer group times but also individually through hierarchical accountability chains.

In a sense, leadership is taken in areas where leadership is needed, and delegated back to the group where it is not. The interesting question is for how long this can last.

1.5 The routinization of charisma and house church leadership

One unfortunate propensity of those house church writers who claim a connection with history is that they seem unwilling to take the implications of history seriously—that is to say, while quick to assert their continuity with the successful side of prior expressions of dynamic Christianity, they are slow to investigate and learn from the social and theological

CHAPTER 1. HOUSE CHURCHES AND LEADERS

factors that led these expressions to 'revert' to being gathered churches, preferring simplistic dismissals—whether it be all Constantine's fault, or a 'lack of faith' leading men to seek refuge in systematization.

Unfortunately for these proponents, however, history shows us that all of the house church movements we have examined so far tend inexorably towards the gathered model, and even if we are to take the claims of external oppression or internal infidelity at their face value, we are left with little reason to believe that such forces will not strike again. As Nigel Wright points out, house churches "are subject to the same problems—what Brunner calls the 'earthly' side of the church: Competition, ambition and the rest of it." (cited in Walker, 1998:18)

But more than this, it is a well-known sociological phenomenon that radical, revolutionary groups generally cannot sustain a charismatic leadership style; "charisma cannot remain stable, but becomes either traditionalized or rationalized, or a combination for both" (Weber et al., 1978:246) Weber's "routinization of charisma", and in particular the concept of the charisma of office, predicts that however dynamic the house church movement may be at any given time, it will tend inexorably towards systematization, and in particular the systematization of leadership.

Applied particularly to the concept of new church movements and denominations, Niebuhr (1975:19–20) sees the routinization of charisma as deriving from the educational and corrective functions of a church:

> By its very nature, the sectarian type of organization is valid only for one generation. The

1.5. The routinization of charisma

> children born to the voluntary members of the first generation begin to make the sect a church long before they have arrived at the years of discretion. For with their coming the sect must take on the character of an educational and disciplinary institution, with the purpose of bringing the new generation into conformity with the ideals and customs which have become traditional.

I would argue that this normative pressure does not merely apply to children. As Niebuhr goes on to say, sectarian groups are often forged in reaction and conflict, and establish norms to emphasise their distinctiveness. Routinization becomes an effective way to ensure compliance with the new norms, and the function of leadership moves quickly from spearheading dynamic change to being both the arbiter of compliance and the deposit of collective wisdom.

We have taken, in this chapter, somewhat of a negative view of house church proponents and their understanding of history; we have also noted that all movements—Christianity itself included—tend inevitably to systematize within a relatively small number of generations, and this generally kills off their vitality. The recurrence, however, of restorationist and revitalization movements throughout history can be seen as an effective and necessary corrective to systematization. Vital and dynamic movements become fossilised, and a new movement forms from their ashes.

From a Christian point of view, we have argued that there is no one divinely ordained form for the church and that all historical expressions of the church have been culturally conditioned. We therefore do not assume that the house church movement as currently expressed, in all its pluriform nature, is anything other than another cultural expression of Christianity—indeed, we have seen the influence of postmodern culture upon its organizational structure—nor should we expect it to avoid the same fate of systematization. However, we see this not as a danger but as an opportunity: an opportunity to remain humble in our advocacy of church forms, and an opportunity for God to bring along a new dynamic form once house churches have themselves systematized. The missiological aim in adopting house churches in Japan is not to spread house churches as an end in itself, for ever and ever, amen, but to find the most *currently* culturally effective form for the spread of the Gospel in that country.

We are therefore prepared to accept the house church style with all of its imperfections, in the absence of anything more perfect and in the anticipation that it will become stale only to be rejuvenated later by another visionary idea.

Or, to put it in the words of the Reformers, *ecclesia semper reformanda*.

1.6 Conclusions: What does leadership mean?

We have looked at a number of factors which have contributed to the understanding of leadership within house churches: the combination of the three trends of apostolic ministry, simple structures and mentoring and coaching.

Turner's definition of the role of an apostle in section 1.3.1 on page 18 is so pivotal to our study that its import

1.6. Conclusions: What does leadership mean?

bears repeating here: he gives a definition of the role of a leader, in a late twentieth-century, Western context, that does not focus on setting strategies, vision or goals, that does not revolve around commanding or even encouraging subordinates, but is focused on the creation and maintenance of group relationships and network linkages.

What is being described is leadership in the postmodern networked organisation, (Tiplady, 2003) where the leader often lacks formal, positional power but provides social cohesion and networking functions. This is a world away from the modernist world's understanding of leadership, which is expressed "mainly in terms of the issuing of orders which are eagerly obeyed by followers whose loyalty is largely determined by the charisma of the leader." (cited in Gill 2006:13) It is even difficult to match up with less autocratic understandings of leadership, such as Kotter's (1990), which still focus on the executive functions of the leader. It is a new and emerging style of leadership for the networked society. Perhaps the closest model we have is what Pulley et al. (2000) call 'e-leadership,' which places the emphasis on "collective tasks and perspectives that move an organization in a particular direction, not individual characteristics or traits."

But it is also the kind of leadership we saw in the New Testament churches, where patronal figures would take responsibility for ensuring group cohesion and well-being while all members of the church would exert influence upon the group; it is the leadership expressed in communitarian societies, as we shall see as we examine Japanese churches specifically.

CHAPTER 1. HOUSE CHURCHES AND LEADERS

Chapter 2

The house church in Japan: its scope and influences

It has been estimated[1] that there are currently around 100 house churches in Japan; we will accept this number as likely, from experience, although note some caveats below. The 2009 survey of Japanese churches (Church Information Service, 2010) reported a total of 7879 churches in Japan, which would mean that at least 1.3% of Japanese churches are of a house church model. While still considerably less than America, where 9% of Protestants attend religious services in a home (Pew Forum, 2009), this is significant for a form of church which has only developed within the last decade in Japan.

To determine more about the scope of the house church in Japan and the understanding of leadership amongst its

[1] Gary Fujino, interview 2009-10-29

members and leaders, a questionnaire (Appendix A on page 101) was distributed to house church leaders. The data in this chapter was derived from the results of this survey and follow-up interviews with house church leaders.

Survey responses were received from 17 leaders from 12 house church networks, between them representing at least sixty-five church groups. (One of the networks surveyed did not keep records on the number of groups; we have not estimated their membership here.) Although a small number of individual respondents, this covers a significant proportion of the churches under investigation and provides useful initial data on the state and ecclesiology of the Japanese house churches.

2.1 History of house church involvement in Japan

A critical period for the house church in Japan seems to have been late 2002 to early 2003. One respondent claimed to have been involved in the Japanese house church movement for 12 years and two others for ten years, but 6 of the 12 networks were founded between 2002 and 2004, with only two networks (those of the Grace Brethren International Missions and Japan Cell Church Mission) founded prior to 2002.

Only one of the missionaries surveyed, from the IMB, planted a house church because of the ecclesiological conviction of their mission agency; the others investigated other forms of church planting before settling on house churches as an intentional strategy for Japan. There were no significant

2.1. History of house church involvement in Japan

distinctions in the survey results between those of missionaries (23% of respondents) and those of national church leaders.

There does not seem to have been any catalytic event to usher in the house church in Japan. One missionary relates what was happening around the 2002–2003 period:

> The vision my wife and I had before coming to Japan was to start house churches, but because of many factors - including our own inexperience!—we weren't realizing those goals. Anyway, around the summer/fall of 2002 out of frustration, I started searching around on the web again seeing what house/cell church resources were out there. I ended up going to Taiwan in November of 2002 for a Cell Church Mission's Network conference. While there, I met some people who were doing house church type work (CPM) ...The next week I met Mitsuo Fukuda [at the Church Planting Institute conference]. In January of 2003, Mitsuo and I went together to Austin, Texas for a Luke 10 training that Tony and Felicity Dale were putting on. Around that same time, Mitsuo was doing an early version of Catalyst Training with several young adults. Some of them started house churches or at least started to head in that direction around that time. Also around that same time, the IMB missionaries (I am not one) started to get top-down instructions that they were to switch to house church planting[2].

[2] Chad Huddleston, interview 2010-07-09

In the previous chapter, we identified missiological interest in Church Planting Movements and the change of strategy of the IMB as drivers for the global house church movement, and here we see these factors in operation in Japan as well. The Church Planting Institute is a ministry of the Japan Evangelical Missionary Alliance, which aims "to see indigenous gospel driven church planting movements fostered in this needy country[3]" and runs training conferences to that end; once again the language of 'church planting movements' appears in a house church context, suggesting a deep link between the two trends. Mitsuo Fukuda is an influential missiologist and house church leader, whose network we will study in more detail in the next chapter.

2.2 Estimating the scope of the house church

There are several reasons why it is difficult and indeed unwise to estimate the scope of the Japanese house church.

First, as we noted in our first chapter, the house church represents a pre-literary culture, and by the nature of the organisational style, detailed membership records and so on are not often kept. If house church proponents' claims are true and groups are multiplying at a rapid rate while laity are being empowered to start new churches in a decentered fashion, it may well be the case that networks cannot be expected to know how many *churches* they have, let alone how many members. (As we have noted, one network could not provide not estimates of their number of churches.)

[3] `http://jcpi.net/`, accessed 2010-07-09

Second, one has reason to be wary of the claims of house church proponents, since well-meaning proponents may, either wittingly or unwittingly, artificially inflate their estimates. This was brought home to me on reading a report (Nacua, 2009) that one house church planter in Japan "has planted over 80 house churches in 2 years!" This is a remarkable claim, and cannot be dismissed simply because it is remarkable; it does accord with the general growth rate claimed by other house church proponents both inside and outside of Japan. Unfortunately, however, in this case the house church planter in question was one of the respondents to my survey and only claims to have seven groups in his network, suggesting that a certain amount of exaggeration has gone on somewhere.

This may not be entirely due to impure motives. Again as we noted in our first chapter, house church organizational principles bring a considerable fuzziness to the definition of the term "church", which may refer to small accountability groups, groups of ten to fifteen people meeting together, a cluster of such groups meeting for periodic celebrations, or entire house church networks.

In our survey, we used the term "meeting groups" in the English questions and "active groups" (活動が盛んなグループ) in Japanese, but even this terminology was apparently unclear. Three respondents from the same network counted themselves as having seven, ten and "four or five" meeting groups. This may be due to differing interpretations of the term, or it may be that members of a loosely-connected network only "see" a particular set of connections relevant to their position, and not necessarily the whole.

Not only this, but precisely when a gathering of individuals becomes a "church" is similarly fuzzy. One respondent said that their network

> probably started around 2006. I joined in 2008. Before that, some friends and families used to meet when I was a student starting in about 2000 but I don't think they had any formal structure. What I mean is that the house church exists as part of every day life, and it's difficult to say when it becomes a "network."

In other words, as well as churches that have been intentionally planted in a house church style, the Japanese house church scene also involves ad hoc Christian gatherings which organically function as house churches; this suggests that the actual scope of house church involvement in Japan is larger than our current estimate, but smaller than some of the more exuberant claims from within the house church movement.

2.3 Ecclesiological characteristics

Our survey showed a number of shared characteristics of house churches. Contrary to my initial assumptions, all but three of the churches surveys had and used a well-known name. One respondent did not know the name of the network, but did know the name of its founder.

All have regular meeting groups, the majority involving singing and Bible study; all but two networks use mentoring of individuals, underlining our assumption in section 1.3.3 on page 22 that mentoring plays a key role in the house church. Indeed, mentoring and discipling are almost seen as coterminous:

> Once, our HC wife was working with a new convert, sharing her life and marriage advice with her on a semi-regular basis. I said that that sounded like good discipleship. And the wife said, I'm not discipling her, Jesus is. When I pointed out that what was doing had elements of discipleship she said that doesn't disciple people, she just shares her life with them.

Five of the twelve networks make use of the "Upwards-Outwards-Inwards" or "Ten-Gai-Nai" schema of house church planting, either in original or modified forms, and a further two networks used portions of the schema for accountability groups. We will examine this influential structure, designed and documented by Fukuda (2010), in the next chapter.

2.4 Survey of leadership understandings

Let us now consider how these churches understand leadership. The first question in this section asked whether the language of "leaders" and "leadership" is used in the churches at all.

Nine of the respondents said that the words were not used at all, or "not particularly", while another used the language of "servants" instead of leaders. One respondent explained the reasoning behind this behaviour:

> The only teacher and leader we have is Jesus. It doesn't make sense to say we have other leaders. Japanese people become co-dependent on leaders and leadership, and there are cases of Christians who want to become leaders to boost their self-image, so we stress that everyone is equal and important. So in that sense everyone is a leader but I've made a point to try not to use the word "leader."

More intriguing were the answers to the next question, where all but one of the churches which *did* speak about "leaders" and "leadership" did *not* have a defined leader for each meeting; conversely, of those church which did not speak about leaders, all but two *were* able to identify a leader for the meeting. This is partly explained by the work of the meeting leader, which was often to choose songs and Bible passages to study, to contact the members, and to facilitate meetings. Sometimes these leaders were chosen by rota:

> Every week the leader is rotated. We've even had it go to my 10 year old son at times (as facilitator). But no one who leads weekly is considered "THE" leader of the church. The leader for that week is only expected to take care of the worship time.

As we shall see in section 4.3 on page 63, choosing a facilitator by rota is an established part of Japanese voluntary society.

There were a variety of responses to the question of the functions of other leaders in the network, but only two of the networks claimed to have no other leaders while a further two reported that "everyone leads". Some saw "other leaders" at what one might call a conceptually higher level than the meeting groups, organising materials and locations, networking with other groups, or forming a council of elders to discuss developments within the groups, while other networks saw other leaders conceptually lower down, assisting the meeting groups:

> The roles are decided naturally: people leading worship, making food, encouraging others, and so on. Each person uses their various giftings. The most important thing is that they hear and obey what God has told them to do... whatever that is is their role for that time.

These "other leaders" often "naturally appear" (3 respondents), are recommended and suggested by others (3 respondents). A deliberately open question asked "what was required for someone to be a leader," allowing repondents either to focus on the nature of individual leaders or on leadership in general. To this, three respondents mentioned the Biblical requirements in 1 Timothy; others mentioned love for God (4 respondents) service, (3 respondents) a clear call, (2 respondents) experience, having followers, "modesty and foresight", "taking responsibility" and "being open."

Seven of the twelve responding networks replied that they had a method for developing leaders, (another network was developing one) based either around Ten-Gai-Nai, Kanto House Church Network's ETA method or "immediate discipleship."

… CHAPTER 2. THE HOUSE CHURCH IN JAPAN

2.5 Conclusions

The restricted scope of this survey naturally constrains the amount one may conclude from this data, and those particularly looking to gain statistical and historical data about the impact and spread of the house church movement in Japan would be well advised to conduct a more extensive survey, especially in light of the diverse and fluid nature of the churches and their purported rapid growth. Nevertheless, we were able to draw some initial conclusions from the data acquired, particularly about the dynamics of their leadership processes.

As predicted, mentoring and leadership development plays a key role in the life of the Japanese house church. While most churches have a leader for their weekly meetings, this is not a static role, often rotating, and is not seen by any church as "the" church leader; it is a functional, facilitatory role. Amongst the more developed house churches with an understanding of leadership training, there is a role for a conceptually higher-level leader, although again not positionally granted, with the function of networking with other groups, being involved in training, and helping to organise church activities. Even those which do not have leadership training, those who are "further along the path" will often take on the discipling of other members.

Leadership, in these churches, is defined primarily in terms of character and active function rather than positional role—indeed, one respondent stated that leadership was a "function, not a designation"—and it is in this sense that everyone can be said to be in leadership.

2.5. Conclusions

Let us now investigate further one of the house churches which responded to the survey, to achieve a deeper understanding of their ecclesiological convictions and how this affects their view on leadership.

CHAPTER 2. THE HOUSE CHURCH IN JAPAN

Chapter 3

Case study: Ten-Gai-Nai churches

In our introduction, we noted that Japanese congregations often "outsource" the work of Christianity to their pastors. Partly this tendency comes from the power distance (see Hofstede, 2005) between pastor and laity which does not leave space for lay involvement, as "Japanese pastors tend to be authoritarian and try to control everything that is happening in their church"(Anketell, 2006:3); partly, this is a general tendency within Japanese religiosity; (explored particularly in Kawano 2005 and Cozens 2010) but partly, the believers do not have an understanding of Christianity as an active, participatory experience and do not have the confidence that they would be able to 'do it right.' (See section D.1 on page 127.)

In order to create rapidly-multiplying, lay-led churches, many Japanese house church leaders have realised the need for a means of explaining the Christian life that is easily grasped, remembered and passed on—perhaps if systematization cannot be avoided, then it can, in some sense, be tamed. Steve Weemes of the Kansai House Church Network has developed a model called ETA, and Mitsuo Fukuda has produced Ten-Gai-Nai, the subject of our investigation.

The aim of the Ten-Gai-Nai schema is that

> the initial training ... takes about two minutes. With a simple plan like that, people only get confused if you talk for too long. For instance, let's say someone's evangelising in a coffee shop and his friend comes to faith. He's practiced sharing these 'guidelines for obeying God' in two minutes, so he can then briefly cover the first part of Christian training by drawing a diagram with a ballpoint pen on the back of a napkin. (See the interview at D.3 on page 135.)

This chapter will examine Ten-Gai-Nai, and in particular attempt to adduce the understanding of leadership underlying the Ten-Gai-Nai model.

As the model has only recently begun to be formally documented, and never before in English, we will consider its nature and development in some detail.

3.1 A sketch of the Ten-Gai-Nai schema

Early drafts of Ten-Gai-Nai circulated as part of Dr. Fukuda's house church training seminars in 2007, but in 2009, he began to write a series of articles explaining the concepts, for serialization in the Revival Japan magazine and eventual publication in book form:

> This New Year, I heard God telling me to write down documents foundational to the movement; I wrote this consciously on my blog, but in July a publisher called me up without any approach from me, and in no time we were making plans to publish a new book.[1]

The philosophical starting-point of Ten-Gai-Nai is that man lives in three fundamental relationships, which we call "upward", "outward" and "inward". This is a rough translation of the Japanese: 'Ten' (天) means 'heaven' (and hence, through Confucian thought, God) whereas 'Gai' (外) and 'Nai' (内) are as much spacial directions as they are social orientations—one's out-group and in-group. (see de Mente, 1994; Nakane, 1972)

The "upward" relationship deals with relationship with God, beginning with what God has done for us and our response of joy and obedience; obedience in particular to loving God and loving neighbour, which leads to the "outward" relationship: to service and evangelism of those outside the church. Evangelism will often be unpopular, frustrating and difficult, but these difficulties produce endurance, and endurance produces character and character produces hope. As a result of this outward orientation, there will be a change in us, which influences our "inward" relationship individually (our relationship with ourselves) and corporately.

[1] Personal correspondence, 2009-09-11.

CHAPTER 3. CASE STUDY: TEN-GAI-NAI CHURCHES

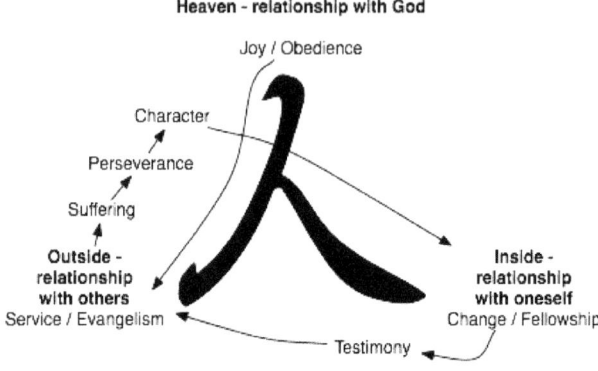

Figure 3.1: The Ten-Gai-Nai schema illustrated via the calligraphic method of writing the Japanese character for 'man'

(banding us together into the people of God) This change also becomes a testimony to others, feeding back into the "outward" orientation. Christianity is seen as the correct handling and balancing of these three relationships.

It is important to note that this is a high-level schema or framework to aid the organisation of thought, rather than a doctrine. The person of Christ, the nature of salvation, understanding of sin and other topics belong to a lower level, expressed within and through this schema. As an example, sin can be defined within the Ten-Gai-Nai framework as a breach of one's responsibilities to rejoice or to obey God, ("upward") anything which could hinder one's witness to others ("outward") or anything which harms personal self-esteem and corporate fellowship. ("inward")

Similarly, church practices are also expressed in Ten-Gai-Nai, often through an interactive, question-and-answer process. For instance, "Ten-Gai-Nai groups" consist of pairs or triplets who meet up once a week for Bible reading, ("upward") intercession for non-Christian friends, ("outward") and sharing and accountability. ("inward") This "inward" sharing is, in a fractal sense, also expressed in terms of guiding questions about the same three relationships; first, there are two questions about the members' "upward" relationships:

- In the past week, when did you feel that God was particularly with you?
- In your Bible reading of the past week, what do you feel that God has been telling you to do and how have you obeyed?

Followed by two questions about their "outward" relationships:

- How have you served others in the past week?
- How have you brought the Gospel to others in the past week?

And finally two questions about their "inward" relationships:

- Have you committed sin in the past week?
- How have you shown love to friends and members of your mission team in the past week?

As well as accountability groups, Fukuda (2010) uses the Ten-Gai-Nai schema to design devotions, 'marriage transformation groups', evangelistic strategies, Bible studies, discipleship and leadership training strategies. (Some of these are outlined in the 'cheat sheet' in appendix B on page 106.)

3.2 Is Ten-Gai-Nai Japanese… and does it matter?

Fukuda willingly admits his borrowings from the "simple church" movement, citing Cole (1999) as a source for his accountability groups and quoting liberally from Dale and Dale (2002), Banks (1990) and Schwarz (1996) in his writings.

This is a considerable shift from Fukuda's early thought. While studying for a Th.M.-Miss. and D.Miss. degrees at Fuller from 1990-1992, his theological focus was on the development of Japanese churches contextualized to the Japanese culture—his Th.M.-Miss. thesis was entitled 'Christian shrines for Japan?' suggesting a fairly radical approach to church structure. His D.Miss. thesis (cited here as Fukuda, 1992) develops this theme, contrasting the Japanese, Hebrew and Western religious paradigms, and suggesting the need for a three-level church structure of one-to-one mentoring and evangelism, small groups which pray for non-believers —here we already see some of the intentionally evangelistic, 'Power Evangelism' style elements of Ten-Gai-Nai groups emerging in Fukuda's thought—and provide opportunity for fellowship and witness, and church services contextualised through various expressions of native religious elements.

In 2002, the think-tank he founded underwent a transformation. 'Mentoring Like Barnabas' (Fukuda, 2002) continued the theme of one-to-one mentoring that appeared in the D.Miss. thesis, apparently influenced by Robert Logan at Fuller, but Fukuda appeared discouraged with contextualization efforts and began to work on a ground-up rethink of church planting.

3.2. Is Ten-Gai-Nai Japanese... and does it matter?

> The major reason why we changed directions stemmed from a strong desire to see New Testament Christianity actualized in Japan. It was discouraging and exhausting to see such little fruit come out of our publications, lectures and conferences. We realized that churches where direct access to God is encouraged and that have a flat and personal relationship structure, rather than hierarchical structures, reflect the lives of people most contextually. ... Both transportation and transplantation are based on the idea of the translation of a model whose starting point is, in the first place, a foreign idea, and which must then be interpreted and then introduced into the native soil. But a fresh incarnation emerges in the soil of a culture where the seed of God's words sprout. (Fukuda, 2005)

For a proponent of radical contextualisation to be advocating lightly-modified variants of Western church planting paradigms may seem a little strange; but in reality, Fukuda is merely doing what the Japanese are renowned for doing so well in the areas of technology and industry: adopting, adapting and refining rather than innovating:

> Even when a simple imitation of a product would suffice, a Japanese is not satisfied with just that. Whether the original is foreign-made or domestically produced, there is a determination to add a new twist that improves the item or modifies its purpose. (Hayashi and Baldwin, 1988:22)

CHAPTER 3. CASE STUDY: TEN-GAI-NAI CHURCHES

To put it in missiological terms, Japanese are inveterate contextualizers! And Ten-Gai-Nai certainly has its 'new twists.' Having attended Fukuda's seminars and heard some of the explanations for particular practices, I can confirm that a lot of thought has been given to 'tweaking' the work of Cole et al. to ensure that they resonate adequately with a Japanese audience while remaining within their general framework and continuing in their overall outward forms. We have seen already the use of Japanese calligraphy and the character for 'man' to provide a metaphor for the connection between the upwards, outwards and inwards orientations. As another example, inductive Bible studies are done with groups broken up into pairs and each member of a pair reports to the group the other member's thoughts on the passage; this is done so that Japanese, who are often uncomfortable sharing their own opinions in public, can share in the privacy of a pair, and then present another person's opinions to the group rather than their own.

In the light of Malone's (2009) experience that 'doing theology with the Japanese'—what we are trying to encourage people to do for themselves using Ten-Gai-Nai as a framework—invariably requires the adoption of concepts (such as a creator God, for instance) from outside of the culture, perhaps we should turn the question around: is Ten-Gai-Nai **un**-Japanese?

After all, Tiplady (2003:60–61) argues that the practice of contextualization, which generally assumes a static and homogenous understanding of culture, makes less sense in a globalized, 'hybridized' and rapidly changing cultural matrix, and I would venture to suggest that few cultures are more hybridized and more rapidly changing than that of Japan. In such a context, the question of what is 'Japanese' and what is not 'Japanese' becomes confused. (see Mathews, 2000)

As it is, 'tweaked' by Dr. Fukuda to avoid being obviously and offensively **un**-Japanese, Ten-Gai-Nai seems as attuned to Japanese culture as any other missiological method—and arguably more so than the Western congregationalist model of church!

3.3 Ten-Gai-Nai leadership development

We can now consider the methods used by Fukuda to train and mentor house church leaders. The main aim of this mentoring is to equip Christians to fulfill all the functions of a Ten-Gai-Nai based house church—evangelism, leading Bible studies, training others, and planting new churches—thus propagating Ten-Gai-Nai down successive generations. This means that training and mentoring methodologies *themselves* also need to be simple and reproducible.

Leadership development in Ten-Gai-Nai is thus done through the same principle of guiding questions as devotions and accountability groups—the questions are simple, open-ended, easy to pass on and cover a wide sphere of personal and ministry life. (See Table 1)

The questions form the core of a training session with the following outline:

> **Prayer** We start by praying to "God who causes the growth" (1 Corinthians 3:7) and ask

Table 3.1: Ten-Gai-Nai leadership development questionnaire

	Past	Present	Future
Upwards Personal	What has God taught you from the Bible in the past week?	When do you particularly have a sense that God is with you?	In what ways will God deepen His relationship with you?
Outwards Personal	Who did you share the Gospel with, and how, in the past week?	Who amongst your non-Christian friends should you be serving, and how?	What can you practically do for the salvation of your friends and family?
Inwards Personal	Reflecting on the past week, is there anything that you need to repent of?	What are you currently wrestling with to help you become more Christ-like?	What choices will help you show love to the believers around you?
Upwards Corporate	How have you helped others to come into an individual relationship with God?	Are your church members holding their devotions and accountability groups?	What is the next step to help your members joyfully follow God?
Outwards Corporate	Please tell me about any people saved in your network within the past month.	How should people be training so that they can improve their relational skills?	What would be needed for you to start a new church?
Inwards Corporate	What sort of things have hampered the unity of your mission team?	What can you do now to help others develop a passion for character building?	What hopes does God hold for the relationships within your team?

for His protection and leading in the coaching session. Also we pray that we would be able to put into practice what we learn from God during the session, and that He would seal out any negative words or attitudes.

Review Looking back on the plan of action that was made at the previous coaching session, we review whether or not we could put that into practice. If we did, then we give thanks and celebrate God's goodness; if not, then we either look at the reasons and revise the aims, or we decide to continue wrestling with it.

Questions With both the coach and the client looking at the questionnaire, the client answers the questions in turn.

Decision We put together a measurable plan of what we want to achieve before the next coaching session, and pray together that we'll be able to achieve it. Then we look back over the session and talk over the most significant parts of it. (Fukuda, 2010)

This scheme, and the mentoring approach in Fukuda 2002, has been critized as trite and lacking in depth[2], and certainly a perfunctory rattling-through of the questions would not comprise an adequate mentoring relationship. However, this is not its intention; it provides a framework

[2] Glenn Myers, personal correspondence

for discussion within the context of a mentoring relationship and allows for those without any experience of mentoring to get started. Naturally some individuals using the scheme will prove to be more probing, more insightful and thus better mentors than others; but that is not the concern of this study. Our concern is to understand what leaders are being produced by this programme and for what purpose they are being developed. We also wish to understand the leadership of this church within the context of Japanese society as a whole. To measure this, we need an understanding of the nature of Japanese leadership and evaluative theories of its development, and this will be the subject of our next chapter.

3.4 What is leadership in Ten-Gai-Nai churches?

One of the movations for this present study was the observation that, although Ten-Gai-Nai groups are designed to be used by facilitators drawn by rota from the membership, and although there is little talk of leadership on a local level, the schema still has a formalized leadership development programme. Why is this, and what kind of leadership are they looking for?

One answer can be found in an article referenced within the Ten-Gai-Nai training manual. (Fukuda, 2010) David Lim writes that

> [t]o start a CPM, you have to be a disciple-maker who knows three basic skills. First, friendship evangelism ...Second, leading disciple-making

> groups ...Third, networking with others ...(Lim, 2009)

It is these skills that define leadership within Ten-Gai-Nai, and these skills which are developed through the mentoring process. Indeed, in responding to the survey, Dr. Fukuda stated that "leaders" within the Ten Gai Nai churches, other than those on the rota to facilitate meeting groups, are responsible for "prayer, training and liaison with other networks"; although not identical to Lim's criteria, these tell us that within the Ten-Gai-Nai stream of church and, I would surmise, within the house church movement more generally, one must not see "leader" as a positional rôle within or above a group, with authority, responsibility, oversight and so on, but more as an example, a person equipped with certain resources and skills that can catalytically transform church groups and the society around them. It is in this sense that Dr. Fukuda states that "everyone can be a leader," and yet there are no positional leaders!

On the other hand, the attitude, displayed both through the survey, through David Lim's quote, and also through the questions in the mentoring questionnaire, is primarily skills-based and secondarily related to group function. As we will see in the next chapter, Japanese leadership theory priorities both performance and group maintainance, but for Christian leadership there is a further dynamic that also remains to be considered; Pilling (2010) argues that Christian mentoring programmes generally major on skills and function but do not intentionally develop Christian character. The Ten-Gai-Nai approach is that character formation is carried out in the context of three-person Ten-Gai-Nai groups (Fukuda 2010, chapter 7), and not necessarily through the mentoring process.

Nevertheless, the role of character in leadership is one we will return to in our final chapter.

3.5 Conclusions

Ten-Gai-Nai is one of the major models for house churches in Japan, with several survey respondents using this methodology to develop or train house church participants. Its simple and fractal structure make it appropriate for fast propagation through a chain of minimally-trained laity. Within this schema, the term "leadership" is used in a non-standard way, to reflect those possessing the basic skills and abilities required for the church to grow and for the scheme to be carried out and propagated. However, we have raised a concern as to whether the content of such leadership adequately includes issues of character formation. Before we address this, however, we will assess this style of leadership against Japanese cultural models.

Chapter 4

Functions of Japanese leadership

Students of Japanese leadership will be aware that, as Fukushige and Spicer (2007) note, "whilst a great deal of literature has investigated Japanese management practices, research on leadership in Japan has been relatively sparse." This chapter aims to review the available literature on leadership practices and theory in Japan. However, due to the constraints of this study, we must be selective in considering only those understandings of Japanese leadership which have direct and obvious application to our theme.

Much of what little research *has* been done on Japanese leadership is explicitly set in the commercial rather than voluntary sectors, and although these studies (particularly Fukushige and Spicer 2007 itself and Yoshioka 2006) present useful evidence about cultural perceptions of leadership, we will only cover them here in passing.

CHAPTER 4. FUNCTIONS OF JAPANESE LEADERSHIP

In order to determine the functions and processes of Japanese leadership, we will survey the literature in two areas: sociological studies of the Japanese people as a whole, and then specifically the sociology of small and voluntary community groups. We will also briefly consider leadership-theoretical understandings of Japanese groups[1].

First we wish to consider the sociological understandings of leadership; that is, the nature of leadership expressed in Japan as distinct from how to measure or improve it, together with cultural considerations which may have given rise to particular dynamics of leadership.

4.1 The group model

Despite its age and its flaws, which we will discuss later, the definitive work on Japanese social intercourse still remains Nakane (1972), which posits that members of a Japanese group have, on the whole, no independent relationship with each other but are all 'rooted' in their vertical relationship with their *oya-bun*. (Literally 'parent part'; patron figure.) The consequence of such a 'rooting' is that the leader is not an external influence upon their group, but is an inseparable part of it. Indeed, the leader is expected to merge their identity with that of the group (p. 72) and cannot avoid developing emotional and personal ties to their *ko-bun* ('child part') subordinates, particularly over an immediate small group.

---

[1]We will not engage in cross-cultural analysis in this study except to note that Korea—whose megachurches show large growth around the strong social capital of an autocratic, Confucian leader (Yang, 2006)—faces similar questions about appropriate leadership structures for new church movements; for which, see Oh (2003).

Hence when Nakane declares that 'Japanese soil cannot grow a charismatic leader,' (p. 74) she is not, as some have suggested, making a negative statement, but a positive one. She is essentially stipulating that within a culture oriented around personal and emotional ties, a dominating leader is undesirable. The effect of charisma is limited to the immediate personal relations, rather than influence directed towards the organisation at large.

Nakane has been criticised (Hendry, 1998; Befu, 1980) for confusing sociology with ideology; Befu argues that Nakane contributes to the field not of sociology but *nihonjinron*, cultural-nationalistic 'writing about the Japanese.' In a sense this criticism is irrelevant: Nakane writes as a Japanese about normative, idealized patterns within her culture. Whether, therefore, such patterns are actually dominant in all Japanese relationships or not, they have value precisely as an indication of what is culturally normative. We therefore accept the group model and the vertical relationship model, but with appropriate reservations about its idealized status. Later we will see theorists who build on this model to provide descriptions of leadership within the Japanese church.

4.2 Diffuse leadership and trust relations

Hirokawa (1982) presents the classical (and therefore now considerably outdated) understanding of Japanese corporate social organisation, particularly within business, from the point of view of internal communication pathways.

He emphasises four components of Japanese management —internal harmony, bottom-up decision making, availability

CHAPTER 4. FUNCTIONS OF JAPANESE LEADERSHIP

of managers and the permanent employment system—and contends that these properties foster free and efficient exchange of information within the organisation.

Hirokawa weaves all of these factors into a safety net which allows for honest and clear communication, as opposed to Western organisations, where mistrust and worry about speaking out of turn serves to inhibit necessary communication. One wonders at this stage whether or not he is falling into the same trap as Nakane: failing to differentiate between making a sociological observation and making a nationalist statement; certainly Hirokawa does not advance empirical evidence to support his beliefs.

From a leadership perspective, Hirokawa considers both the physical and social availability of leaders to their subordinates. He surmises that the job of a leader is to develop social networks which create a web of trust within the organisation, and to create relationships which extend their influence far beyond matters concerning the workplace.

It is important to note that Japanese culture is not static, and the attitudes of workers towards these diffuse relationships is changing as Matsumoto (2002:137) records:

> As workers begin to draw sharper distinctions between their personal lives and work, the boundaries between self and family on the one hand and work, company, colleagues on the other become greater. Efforts by superiors to intervene in the lives of their subordinates are more often than before being looked upon as interference or an intrusion of privacy...As

Japanese culture continues to change, management and leadership style will surely continue to evolve as well.

However, based on personal experience, I would say that diffuse relationships still form the basis of Japanese perceptions of leadership, and that even churches—at least gathered churches— would qualify as "work" rather than "personal life" for the purposes of these social relationships: the patron relationship applies as much between pastor and laity as it does between superior and subordinate at work. At one point my Japanese pastor, acting in his patron role, called me in to discuss the state of my gardening, after he had received complaints from neighbours—an exercise of diffuse authority which would be unthinkably intrusive from a Western perspective!

Does this apply to the house churches, lacking as they do the formal structure of gathered churches? For the present, house churches are closer to the "personal life" than the "work" model, but our argument in section 1.5 on page 25 was that house churches inevitably take on an organisational structure at some point, and thus when formal leadership characteristics emerge, we should expect them to follow the dominant pattern of society—diffuse, patronal relationships.

In a similar vein to Hirokawa's paper, Taka and Foglia (1994) contrast idealized Japanese organisations and Western organisations, and consider why Japanese organisations suffer less from ethical problems. They highlight three *spiritual* factors key to Japanese leadership style:

(1) emphasis on self-realization, (2) appreciation of diverse human abilities, and (3) trust in others.

CHAPTER 4. FUNCTIONS OF JAPANESE LEADERSHIP

According to Taka and Foglia, these three factors arise from the fact that Japanese society is permeated by two normative environments: the transcendent environment which "assumes that all persons and things transcend day to day existence by being linked to a higher force", which provides self-actualization for the whole society, and a similar normative environment which provides self-actualization for societal groups.

For our purposes, we will focus on two aspects of Taka and Folgia's argument. First, their definition of the ideal leader is one "who permits or encourages others to proceed to the life force through their own work." Appreciating the role and importance of each person's specialism leads to an appreciation of their understanding for the challenges of their work, and hence a belief that the worker knows best how to improve and refine the working experience.

Second, and flowing from this, comes the fundamental trust a leader expresses in his subordinates. Trusting others is an opportunity for the leader to earn trust themselves, which is required for group cohesion and solidarity. While trust is obviously a necessary dynamic in Western understandings of leadership—Maxwell (1998:61) calls it the "foundation of leadership"—the focus is mainly on the trust that subordinates have in a leader. The Japanese practice of trusting followers to do their jobs best would qualify as *laissez-faire* leadership in the West, a style of leadership which would be contraindicated by Western models. (See, e.g. Avolio and Bass 1991.) While this process rings true for industry, it is interesting to note that, as we have seen, pastors in Japanese churches are often seen as controlling and unwilling to trust their parishioners. (Anketell, 2006:3)

This is likely due to the tendency in most Japanese relationships towards co-dependence, documented clearly by Doi (2002). In this sense, it may well be that the *ideal* leader is catalytical and *laissez-faire*, but other cultural constraints restrict the leader's ability to achieve that ideal.

4.3 Sociology of voluntary organisations

It is our contention that the house church, as a voluntary association (following Ramseyer below), has more in common with the voluntary sector than with the commercial sector, and hence to provide insights into Japanese leadership and group dynamics which can apply usefully to the house church environment, we must investigate the well-established Japanese network of voluntary organisations and the literature surrounding such organisations.

Japanese society is permeated by interlocking networks of voluntary associations: neighbourhood groups, community development groups, non-profit organisations, hobby circles, parent-teacher associations and so on (Bestor, 1985). In many cases, leadership of such organisations is determined by rota or lottery, rather than perceived ability (Imamura, 1993:9). The literature concerning these organizations is scattered around the fields of sociology, urban planning, local government and so on, and hence has been approached from a number of analytical angles and methodologies. We will not endeavour to undertake a comprehensive survey of these sources, but focus on aspects of leadership relevant to house churches.

Ramseyer (1995), writing from a missiological perspective, highlights the patron-client relationship as playing "a

CHAPTER 4. FUNCTIONS OF JAPANESE LEADERSHIP

decisive role in the networks that hold society together in Japan" but also provides an interesting insight which is missed by other sociological commentators: he explores the difference between natural groups, where membership is decided by social identity—work, family, the nation and so on—and voluntary associations. Natural groups are seen as corporate identity to which the individual is subordinate, whereas voluntary groups are an extension of the individual and hence subordinate to the corporate will. For Japanese, therefore, if there were a clash of responsibilities on a Sunday morning, for example, it would be incontrovertible that going to work (one's social identity) would take precedence over church meetings. (a voluntary association)

Ramseyer does not elaborate on differences in leadership between the two types of group, other than mentioning that the authority of the leader is emphasised in traditional, natural groups more than in voluntary assocations; in a sense, one cannot evade the leadership of a natural group without "dropping out" of one's social responsibilities, but one can easily walk away from a voluntary group, so their expression of leadership must be more tentative.

Ramseyer's other important contribution is to connect the concept of the vertical society to Christian leadership: the pastor 'owns' the church, the church is not connected horizontally to other churches, and believers are anchored to each other only by their relationship to the pastor. This explains many aspects of Japanese church leadership: the upheaval that comes when a missionary hands a church over to a pastor, (restructuring from Western-style horizontal ties to vertical ties) when one pastor succeeds another (the church

4.3. Sociology of voluntary organisations

frequently splits because its allegiance is to the pastor, not the community[2]) and the lack of co-operation between churches.

Although Ramseyer does not say so explicitly, the relationship between clergy and laity in gathered churches is more that of *sensei-deshi* (master and apprentice) than of boss and staff. Writing before the advent of the house church in Japan, Ramseyer's work seeks to describe leadership dynamics within the church as a hybrid between voluntary-associative and hierarchical institutions. Ramseyer's paper is useful as far as it goes but to truly understand leadership in the house churches from a social-theoretical point of view, it must be developed further to include a deeper treatment of the nature of non-hierarchical affinity groups.

First, what place does the house church find within the understanding of Japanese voluntary associations? Fujimoto and Nakase (2000) posit a two-dimensional taxonomy of community groups in Japanese society, following a study of voluntary associations in the Tamba area of Hyogo prefecture. Their dimensions are local community focus versus theme focus, and independent democracy organization versus government co-operation. Under this schema, house churches would be theme-focused independent democratic groups, known in Japanese as 'circles', (サークル) so let us investigate the sociology of the circle in more detail.

Kobayashi (2007) uses the case study of an art circle to investigate the development of social capital in circles, and cites a Japanese Cabinet Ministry's report on the necessary conditions for such development:

---

[2]How such a communitarian culture can prioritize loyalty to the individual rather than the group is yet to be understood, and is perhaps a key consideration for our purposes.

- An element of discovery or pioneering
- An element of leadership or co-ordination which works to build interpersonal relationships
- An element of open, public communication[3]

To this end, the Cabinet office's report encourages

the existence of rules for activities within the circle which encourage open, flat networks... widening of networks based on trust relationships...[and] promoting the formation of mutual trust between members and those external to the group. [4]

---

[3] From p. 9:
「先駆性あるいは課題発見力の要素」「人間関係づくりを行なうリーダーシップあるいはコーディネーターの要素」「コミュニケーションのための公共空間の要素」を有することが求められている。

[4] From p. 9:
水平的でオープンなネットワークを醸成するための活動のルール(規範)の存在や、市民活動が社会的な成果の実現につながり、市民活動の更なる活発化(信頼関係に基づくネットワークの広がり)などの好循環を導き出すこと、および、橋渡し型ソーシャル・キャピタル培養器としての積極的な活動展開、外部の人・組織との相互信頼形成の促進などが課題として 指摘されている。

From this we can see the connection between the concepts of leadership in a 'circle' and the building of networked relationships. The job of the leader is to create a "favourable climate" (好循環) for group cohesion and actively encouraging widening of the group's trust relationships.

This understanding of leadership within (secular) social circles in Japanese tallies well with current Christian thinking on missional communities: that leaders must focus the community on its external relationships as well as its internal relationships, and that there should be a "tension between the visionary and the relational, team-building elements of leadership." (Cray, 2009:133) This tension is echoed by Kado (2008), who argues that the ideal community leader should have "limited liability", and should be able to provide group traction, develop a variety of individual leaders under them, and also promote the widening of external relationships by diversifying the group's activities around its central core.

Ōtsubo's (1998) investigation into the Japanese "cultural movement" examines the post-war boom in voluntary associations in Japanese society. In a summary of his findings, (Ōtsubo 1990) he gives four necessary conditions for the development of such associations:

> First, the circle will not develop unless there is respect for the wishes of its members and democratic operation. ... Second, the circle will not develop unless its viewpoint shifts from being "a good use of leisure time" to "acquiring a right perspective on life and society." ... Third, the circle's development is dependent upon efforts both internally and externally, that

CHAPTER 4. FUNCTIONS OF JAPANESE LEADERSHIP

is, the betterment of social conditions. ... Fourth, there is the necessity of developing teaching and learning to further these aims[5].

Such a description should provide reassurance to the developers of Japanese house church systems such as Ten-Gai-Nai that their efforts are on the right track; it explicitly connects leadership, training, an external social focus, and the development and propagation of the group.

To summarize, our study of voluntary groups has centralized the concepts of trust relationship networks and the widening of external activities. It is worth pausing for a moment to note that this understanding of leadership is not something that would normally be found in Western textbooks on the subject!

---

[5] From p. 84:

第1は、成員の要求の尊重とサークルの民主的運営がなければサークルは発展しないということー「サークルの民主的運営」に関わる点である。第2は、「余暇善用」のサークル観から「生活と社会を見つめ、正しいものの見方を身につける」サークル観に移らなければサークルは発展しないことー「余暇善用型の克服」の課題である。第3は、サークルの発展はサークル内部の努力とともに、外部、すなわち社会的条件を有利にすることも必要であることー「社会的条件の獲得」に関わる点である。第4は、これらを遂行して行くために不可欠な教育学習の発展ー「学習内容の科学化」である。

4.4 Leadership theory

Finally, let us consider the contributions of the emerging field of leadership theory in Japan. Although we have noted the space constraints it is instructive to briefly consider empirical investigations of Japanese leadership, building on the theoretical frameworks we have gathered from sociological study and testing them against survey and study data.

Fukushige and Spicer (2007) begin by applying Bass and Avolio's 'full-range leadership model' to Japan, testing the hypothesis that the preference for transformational over transactional leaders is universal. Through an admittedly small-scale series of interviews with Japanese followers, they discovered that the most effective leadership styles under Bass and Avolio's model actually received little endorsement as an ideal style.

Almost all respondents showed a preference for protective and network styles of leadership. Most respondents believed that social activities with their leaders (so called 'after-five') were beneficial but relatively infrequent. Many of the values that they uncovered, particularly liberalism, trust, punctuality, use of network ties, protection and 'after-five' styles, are not considered by American leadership theories and thus should form part of an integrated theory of Japanese leadership.

How would such styles apply to church leadership in general and to non-hierarchical church in particular? First, it suggests that the networked nature of house churches is a culturally appropriate organisational form. Second, non-hierarchical churches differ from gathered churches in terms of power distance. As we have seen, the leader of a gathered church acts at a high power distances from the laity, and both trust and 'after-five' elements are lacking. Where the power distance is lower in house church styles, due to the leadership not occupying a privileged position, social activities and trust are easier to maintain.

A similar attempt to apply American leadership theories to Japanese society is provided by Yoshioka (2006). This study tests Japanese subordinates' preferences against the Situational Leadership model suggested by Hersey and Blanchard. Building on previous studies by Hayashi and Matsubara (1998) and Takahara and Yamashita (2004), Yoshioka found that

> [t]he leadership style which Japanese people wanted their leader to exhibit was both higher relationship behavior and higher task behavior than the Situational Leadership model suggested.

Yoshioka then goes on to modify the Situational Leadership model for use in Japan, by increasing both the relationship and task behaviour metrics of leadership behaviour; in short, the model was restricted to two classifications rather than the original four, with lower-readiness subordinates best satisfied with the S2 (Selling) style and higher-readiness subordinates responding best to the S3 (Participating) style. Telling and Delegating were contraindicated.

This naturally impacts upon house church leaders as it suggests that such leadership needs to be personally involved: as Nakane's theory predicted, Japanese leaders ideally sit within a group rather than over and above it. Systems such as

4.4. Leadership theory

Ten-Gai-Nai which seek to democratise leadership and reduce power distance by making leadership a matter for all members help to increase the relationship behaviour of leaders.

On the other hand, this relational activity should not be at the expense of task focus. A leader is not merely a social facilitator; as much as this role is important, the leader must facilitate the group towards the achievement of particular ends.

Kawazoe (2007) is an empirical study of idealized leadership within Japanese non-profit organisations. In her surveys, she found that some of the traditional characteristics of Japanese management predicted by Hirokawa and Taka and Foglia—bottom-up decision making, delegation to specialists and so on—were contraindicated in the case of non-profit organisations. Instead, emphasis was placed on the personability of the leader. Her conclusion is that the ideal type of leadership for non-profits is democratic leadership, which echoes Ōtsbuo's findings, but also that not merely the group leader but all members of the group must have an awareness of the role of leadership, and that such awareness should permeate both individual and group activity.

The primary Japanese-born theory of leadership is expressed by Misumi (1995). At the urging of Kurt Lewin, Dr. Kanoe Sakamoto of Kyushu University began to test the generality of Lewin et al.'s (1939) leadership theory. Jyuji Misumi then extended these tests, carrying out wide-scale research on over 5,000 Japanese workers and managers, and analysed the results according to two metrics: Performance (or 'P'), and Maintenance ('M'). Performance is concerned with the achievement of goals, particularly goals relevant to the work group; Maintenance is concerned with the cohesion of

CHAPTER 4. FUNCTIONS OF JAPANESE LEADERSHIP

the work group. The original paper which proposed the theory (Misumi, 1964) explains the distinction as follows:

> Assuming three types of leadership, P, M, and PM, we experimentally analyzed their relationship with the productivity of the group. P-type corresponds to conventional "autocratic" or "work-centered" type. M-type corresponds to "democratic" or "human-relation-centered" type, and PM-type is both work and human relation centered.

While this may appear superficially similar to the transactional and transformational measures of leadership, there are two major distinctions: the first is that transformational-transactional is seen as a continuum scale, whereas P and M factors reinforce each other; in this sense it is similar to Blake and Mouton's (1964) "managerial grid" model. The second is the emphasis on maintaining group function and internal cohesion, rather than providing consideration for individual followers as in Western models. Ideal leaders were found to combine P and M functions.

Once again we see the emphasis on group maintenance as a critical function of Japanese leadership. Misumi's theory (backed up by numerous studies; see Seki et al. 1992; Smith et al. 1989) finds that ideal leaders in Japan are those who both ensure that goals are achieved and production maintained, and that the social needs of the group are met.

4.5 Areas of omission and future work

As we noted in the introduction, the field of leadership theory in Japan is in its infancy. We have examined the literature from two major perspectives: the sociological perspective of how groups of Japanese people behave, and the leadership perspective which provides frameworks for measuring and understanding leadership preferences. What we are not currently seeing is any work to bridge the two areas: to explain why particular behaviours are preferred within the particular sociological milieu of Japan.

In part, this is a natural consequence of the recency of leadership studies as a research area in Japan, but it may also prove to be because the relevant literature is scattered across multiple disciplines, from sociology, public policy, nursing, and even landscape architecture, (Fujimoto and Nakase, 2000) and cross-disciplinary communication in Japanese academia is famously rare. (van Wolferen, 1990:238)

Within the church, we have not seen any Japanese writers (with the perennial exception of Fukuda 1993) grapple with contextualizing the nature of church governance and organization for Japan, nor develop a Japanese viewpoint on Christian leadership. There is little evidence that Japanese Christians are appropriating surrounding cultural understandings of voluntary assocations, but seeing themselves primarily within inherited congregationalist models. (Cozens, 2006)

All of these areas would benefit from further research to tie together disparate understandings of leadership within the Japanese church.

4.6 Evaluation

If we were to summarize the findings of our survey of Japanese leadership tendencies, it would be in the words "social cohesion." Leaders are makers, shapers and maintainers of group unity, and the primary function of a Japanese leader is to provide the appopriate social environment for a group's functioning.

We see this in Hirokawa's social understanding of Japanese leadership as group trust-making, and in Fukushige and Spicer's emphasis on trust and on the "after-five" activities of a team; we see it in Taka and Foglia's understanding of "group cohesion and solidarity"; we also see it in Performance-Maintenance theory's stress on the need for idealized leaders in the Japanese context to be able to maintain and facilitate group cohesion. Ramseyer also identifies "keeping the group together" as the most important function of the leader, and all of the other commentators on voluntary organizations emphasise the leader as the builder of networked relationships within the group.

This idea of providing group unity is, in a sense, not entirely unlike the *paterfamilias* approach to leadership we saw in the New Testament churches in section 1.1.1 on page 7—indeed, Ramseyer explicitly identifies the patron-client nature of Japanese social relations. In both cases, the leader's main function is the maintainance of social cohesion through adequate managing of group relationships. Perhaps this commonality points towards a more general understanding of leadership within communitarian cultures. In our next chapter, we will consider the appropriateness of this style of leadership to the church in Japan and the house churches in particular.

Chapter 5

What is leadership in Japanese house churches?

Both our surveys and our sociological study have led us towards a new understanding of leadership in Japanese house churches. First, the nature of "leadership" itself is not what Western readers may be used to. When referring to Japanese house churches—and, as we shall go on to argue, postmodern organisational structures in general—we must first dispense with what Witzel (2007) calls the 'dyadic' model of leadership, where some *are* leaders and some not; there is no distinct class of leaders over and above a second distinct class of followers. Instead, leadership is a quality that some *have*; or rather, that everyone has to varying degrees. This leadership does not mean "the mature use of power to enable others to achieve higher goals" (Barr and Barr, 1994:17) nor is it "the process of

CHAPTER 5. CONCLUSION

moving a group in some direction through mostly noncoercive means." (Kotter, 1988:5) In the case of networks using the Ten-Gai-Nai schema, it is the quality of being proficient in the house church skillset and able to train others in those skills; it is a function primarily of knowledge and achievement rather than power. Admittedly those skills are, on the whole, social, and require the ability to influence people, but the leadership expressed is neither positional nor directive. Indeed, one could replace the word "leadership" with "disciple-making ability" without great loss of meaning.

Second, we have found that based on the key concept of social cohesion, Japanese house church leadership involves maintaining and developing relationships, mentoring and training church members in the principles of church multiplication, networking with others, and ensuring that, as Feddes (2008) puts it, the needs of the family are met. In the case of the Bridge of Hope networks, leadership is, in true *paterfamilias* style, correlated with hospitality. At this point at least, the modern house churches do resemble their New Testament namesakes.

Let us conclude this study by assessing this leadership style against the dominant concerns of the church: whether this style is a good fit with the wider cultural context, whether it actually meets the needs of the churches, and whether it has anything from which the wider church community, both inside Japan and outside, can learn.

5.1 Fit with Japanese leadership functions

To assess house church leadership against the backgroup of leadership within Japanese society as a whole, we will use Taka and Foglia's (1994) definition of a leader as "who permits or encourages others to proceed to the life force through their own work."

We choose this definition because, as well as applying to the classic Japanese enterprise manager, it fits well with the voluntary sector definitions of leadership we encountered in the previous chapter. It is also close to the 'catalyst' role for leadership in non-hierarchical organisations in the West, as highlighted in Brafman and Beckstrom (2006:109): the leader who brings others into contact in a network and then retreats, allowing them to, as it were, "proceed to the life force through their own work."

Certainly the form of house church mentoring described by Fukuda (2002) is a catalytic process, with the mentor providing support for the vision and ambition of the mentee; Fukuda distinguishes this from what he sees as traditional Japanese styles of encouragement and coaching which, contrary to Taka and Foglia, emphasise reliance and co-dependency. (See also Doi 2002.) In this sense, perhaps the style of leadership involved in the house churches is closer to the cultural ideal of Japanese leadership than is commonly found in the business world!

As well as catalytical leadership, the function of connecting with external groups is also emphasised by Kobayashi (2007) in her analysis of the networking role of leaders; since several of our survey respondents highlighted the need for higher-level leaders to network with other groups, we see this cultural dynamic at work within the house churches as well.

Hence we may conclude that although the forms of the house churches have been received partially from Western sources such as Simson (2001) and Cole (1999), their leadership functions are not out of place with the ideals already found within Japanese society. We will later argue that one reason for this is that these ideals are converging with the ideals of leadership within the postmodern organisation in the West.

5.2 Fit with ecclesiological self-understanding

We have summarised the Japanese conception of leadership as the promotion of social cohesion. Leadership in the house churches follows this model, with all members bearing part of the responsibility for the functioning of the group as a whole. In terms of the functions performed in Japanese house church leadership, let us now return to Turner's definition of the function of an apostle (quoted in section 1.3.1 on page 18) within his context, the Restorationist churches of the UK, as this proves a very close fit with what we have seen of the functions in our house churches.

First, an apostle was responsible for promoting the internal unity and rise to maturity of individual congregations. We see this on a micro-scale inside the churches as all members have the leadership responsibility of mentoring and discipling those who have lesser faith experience than themselves. Apostles also are responsible for promoting visible unity between groups, which as we have seen is an essential part of Japanese voluntary organisation leadership; finally, apostles provide the link between different apostolic works, in a networking relationship, which was also identified as a function of leadership by some of our survey respondents.

In short, the experience of the UK house churches in the 1960s provides a useful model for understanding the leadership expressed in Japanese house churches. Similar ecclesiological pressures have resulted in similar forms and hence similar functions of leadership. Indeed, one might say that when it comes to church leadership, in a reversal of Sullivan's (1896) dictum, function follows form—small groups designed for every-member ministry require the kind of leadership functions that we see in the Japanese house church.

In this sense, the leadership patterns expressed in the house churches are not so much a good fit with their ecclesiological self-definition but the natural result of it.

5.3 Applicability to wider church community

Ramseyer's paper on the patron-client relationship is an important bridge point for us because it draws together some of the themes we have discovered about house churches within the context of the gathered Japanese church. We will analyse two of these themes in attempting to apply lessons from the house church to the gathered church.

First, the house churches challenge the gathered churches in terms of their empowerment of the laity. Often conceived

CHAPTER 5. CONCLUSION

as a reaction against the clericalism of Japanese gathered churches, the house churches make every-member ministry a conscious and explicit goal. Where Ramseyer sees the gathered church operating within the structures of the vertical society, house churches seek to break down vertical relationships in a conscious attempt to avoid hierarchy, and its associated problems (from an every-member-ministry point of view) of passivity and co-dependence.

Second, the house churches raise important questions as to what degree the *gathered* churches operate their leadership and government in a way that makes sense for a Japanese voluntary association. As we have seen, there is a close connection between the house church's definition of a leader as a networking relationship-maintainer and the role of a leader in a circle or social group as identified by Kobayashi *et al*; but the gathered churches tend to use a more Western model of church leadership. (Anketell, 2006) In particular, Kado's conception of a "limited liability" leader is almost entirely absent, with the pastor exercising almost absolute personal power over the church. (Braun, 1971)

In an earlier paper (Cozens, 2010) I argue that this factor is partly connected to the Japanese exaltation of the teacher role, and the association of clergy as a religious teacher, but in both of these areas, the house churches challenge the gathered churches both to rediscover the concept of 'pastor' in its original meaning of shepherd and servant of the flock, and to connect that role more closely with the more network-based leadership of similar kinds of voluntary association in Japan such as the circle or the non-profit organisation.

Finally, do the Japanese house churches have anything to say to church government outside of Japan? I believe that they do.

5.3. Applicability to wider church community

In our analysis of house church leadership, we have been able to trace a straight line from the *paterfamilias* leadership of the New Testament house churches, through the network-connection understanding of apostleship in UK house churches in the 1960s, to the emerging house churches in Japan today. As we have previously noted, this is a very different definition of leadership to that found in most Western Christian literature, which emphasises vision, direction and so on.

But perhaps the prevalent thought in the West on church government, and on leadership more generally, is actually a temporary aberration against the longer historical mainstream of leadership-as-relationship-management—albeit an aberration which has lasted for two centuries. Certainly the overarching metaphor of command and control which permeates Western leadership thought reflects the mechanization of the Industrial Revolution. (Morgan, 2006) As we move into a post-industrial society, with its renewed emphasis on human relationship, (Holt, 1995:19) perhaps we shall see a shift in the notion of church leadership similarly away from the vision-and-encouragement model and more towards what the Japanese are already doing in terms of relationship management. (see Barna, 2001:56)

We have already seen the rise of the networked organisation as a new model for church and mission, (Tiplady, 2003:112ff.) which will require a new set of leadership skills—those who are used to wielding considerable power and influence within their own organisation may find it difficult to adjust to an order in which achieving their goals requires a much higher degree of co-ordination with other organisations. At the same time, postmodernity places a high emphasis on personalization and individual choice, (Herangi, 2002:3–5) and successful leaders of postmodern church structures will need to be able to, in Taka and Foglia's (1994) words again, "permit or encourage others to proceed to the life force through their own work;" in other words, take into account the diversity of individual choice and thereby trust the specializations of their subordinates, something which Taka and Foglia identify as a key factor in Japanese leadership style. Leaders operating in this model will tend to be catalytical, rather than positional, and will increase an organisation's effectiveness through their ability to network those of different specializations and thereby giving others the space for synergy, as described by Brafman and Beckstrom (2006).

It is therefore my contention that successful leadership patterns within the Japanese house church would provide a useful model for leadership within non-Japanese forms of church, in particular the more postmodern, emergent expressions of church in the West, and eventually more widely as Western church patterns are gradually reshaped by their prevailing cultural context. We will, I surmise, be looking to ideas such as those of Ōtsubo (1998), Kado (2008) and Kobayashi (2007) to develop a renewed model for leadership in this milieu.

5.4 Critiques and improvements

If there is an area in which the Japanese church can grow, it is in a lacuna from which the Western churches also suffer (Pilling, 2010)—that in making leadership essentially skills-based, the conception of leadership as exemplary moral character, and

5.4. Critiques and improvements

thus the need for mentoring and intentional development of Christian character, becomes less marked.

Certainly in the case of Ten-Gai-Nai, the emphasis on the democratisation of leadership and the priesthood of all believers—while an essential response to the extreme clericalisation of the Japanese church—needs to be counterbalanced against Biblical demands on leaders' character. (1 Timothy 3, for instance, which three of the survey respondents mentioned as a requirement for leadership.) Even within the emerging churches in the UK, mentoring for leadership is primarily about church planting skills rather than deep character issues. (See, for instance, Hopkins and Hedley 2008)

As we have seen, leadership can be correlated with proficiency in the house church multiplication skillset, and the questions used in leadership development process within Ten-Gai-Nai are primarily goals- and outcomes-based, with the aim of greater church multiplication. In Misumi's terms, preferred house church leadership emphasises both Performance (planting more churches) and Maintenance (meeting the needs of the family) axes, but as Christians we need to add a third axis, that of Character. While the Ten-Gai-Nai approach is to trust in the Holy Spirit's internal transformation as a natural result of ministry, (see Fukuda 2010, ch. 2) this process needs to be explicitly celebrated and incorporated as a consciously introspective element of leadership development.

Secondly, there may be a sense in which the reaction against hierarchy goes too far. The New Testament certainly does speak of leaders, and indeed shortly after Paul's requirements for the character of elders in 1 Timothy 3—and the fact that there is a separate standard for elders over and above ordinary congregants is a tacit admission that there *is* indeed a distinction between elders and ordinary congregants—we see Paul in 1 Timothy 5 write that "Elders who provide effective leadership must be counted worthy of double honor, especially those who work hard in speaking and teaching;" (v. 17) his next verse is widely interpreted as a call for the establishment of a salaried leadership (Guthrie 1990:117– 118, Fee 1988:128; see also Wright 2004) or at the very least, (Marshall and Towner, 1999:614) some form of material compensation.

Those networks which claim not to have any leadership, or to place all believers on the same level, are therefore not as in line with the Biblical pattern as they may claim; as a state of reaction against a particular cultural phenomenon, what they do is essential, but as a permanent state, it is unsustainable. However, as we have argued in section 1.5 on page 25, natural forces of the routinization of charisma would suggest that the current unstable situation will "normalize" into a structured leadership at some point in the future.

5.5 Areas for future study

As with any phenomenon in its infancy, giving a long-term prognosis is difficult. It may be that the house church in Japan proves to be a passing fad, or that, like the British house church movement, systematizes to form a new set of fairly traditional denominations; less likely, it may maintain its current character. This study has been an attempt to take a preliminary look at the nature of these house churches and to understand how their leadership structures operate. Further study will be necessary as the movement develops and changes.

5.5. Areas for future study

In particular, we can anticipate that the movement will continue to struggle with pressures of a co-dependent social environment (Doi, 2002) and a natural tendency in Christian structures towards conformity and orthodoxy. (Niebuhr, 1975) To what degree the various networks develop strategies for mitigating this pressure and maintaining their nature will be a critical factor in the growth and vitality of the movements. A diachronic study would therefore be necessary to assess the development of the house church networks and the effect on their ability to maintain every-member ministry.

Second, our survey is restricted both in its scope by its size but also because the answers have come from leaders and founders of house church networks. It is possible that these answers therefore reflect the ideals of the house church movement rather than the reality. Our study has provided useful conclusions about the nature of that idealized leadership, but more study is required to understand to what degree house churches fulfill their ambitions.

Finally, we have already noted (in section 2.2 on page 34) that there are methodological difficulties in estimating the size of the house church movement in Japan. A wider survey, backed by fieldwork, would be useful in determining more about the scope of this intriguing new movement.

CHAPTER 5. CONCLUSION

Bibliography

Titles given in square brackets are the author's translation of Japanese titles.

Anketell, S. (2006). Cell groups at Tsuda church, *Japan Christian Link News* (Spring 2006).

Avolio, B. and Bass, B. (1991). *The full range of leadership development*, Binghamton, NY: Center for Leadership Studies.

Banks, R. (1990). *Going to Church in the First Century*, Jacksonville, FL: Seedsowers.

Barna, G. (2001). *Real Teens*, Ventura: Regal Books.

Barnett, M. (2007). Why do house churches and small groups persist throughout church history?, *in* R. Zdero (ed.), *Nexus: The World House Church Movement Reader*, Pasadena, California: William Carey Library, chapter 14, pp. 161–166.

Barr, L. and Barr, N. (1994). *Leadership Development: Maturity and Power*, Austin, Texas: Eakin Press.

Befu, H. (1980). A critique of the group model of Japanese society, *Social Analysis* (5/6): 29–43.

Bestor, T. (1985). Tradition and Japanese social organization, *Ethnology* **24**(2): 121–135.

Blake, R. and Mouton, J. (1964). *The Managerial Grid: The Key to Leadership Excellence*, Houston: Gulf Publishing Company.

Boff, L. (1986). *Ecclesiogenesis: The Base Communities Reinvent the Church*, London: Collins.

Bosch, D. (1991). *Transforming mission: Paradigm shifts in theology of mission*, Maryknoll, NY: Orbis books.

Bovet, F. and Seed, T. A. (1896). *A Pioneer of Social Christianity: Count Zinzendorf*, Stoke-on-Trent: Harvey & Tait UK.

Brafman, O. and Beckstrom, R. (2006). *The Starfish And the Spider: The Unstoppable Power of Leaderless Organizations*, London: Penguin.

Braun, N. (1971). *Laity mobilized: Reflections on Church growth in Japan and other lands*, Grand Rapids, MI: Eerdmans.

Bulley, C. J. (2000). *The Priesthood of Some Believers: Developments from the General to the Special Priesthood in the Christian Literature of the First Three Centuries*, Carlisle, Cumbria: Paternoster Press.

Church Information Service (2010). 日本の教会について知りたい方へ [For those who want to know about the Japanese church], http://www.church-info.org/html/churchmap.html, accessed 2010-05-21.

Cole, N. (1999). *Cultivating a Life for God: Multiplying Disciples Through Life Transformation Groups*, Signal Hill, CA: CMA Resources.

Cozens, S. (2006). *Contextual leadership development training for Japanese Christians*, BA Research Paper, Ware: All Nations Christian College.

Cozens, S. (2010). *Clergy and laity in the background of Japanese religiosity*, Presentation notes for MAA1 course, Gloucester: Redcliffe College.

Cray, G. (ed.) (2009). *Mission-shaped Church*, London: Church House Publishing.

Dale, T. and Dale, F. (2002). *Simply Church*, Austin, TX: Karis.

de Mente, B. L. (1994). *NTC's Dictionary of Japan's Cultural Code Words*, Lincolnwood, IL: NTC Publishing Group.

Doi, H. (2002). *The Anatomy of Dependence*, 2nd edn, Tokyo: Kodansha.

Eckhardt, J. (1999). *Moving in the Apostolic*, Ventura: Gospel Light Publications.

Feddes, D. J. (2008). Caring for God's household: a leadership paradigm among New Testament Christians and its relevance for church and mission today, *Calvin Theological Journal* 43(2): 274–299.

Fee, G. D. (1988). *1 and 2 Timothy, Titus*, Peabody, Massachusetts: Hendrickson Publishers.

Fowlkes, D. (2004). *Developing a Church Planting Movement in India*, PhD thesis, University of Free State.

Fujimoto, M. and Nakase, I. (2000). 兵庫県丹波地域における住民グループ活動の実態把握に☒☒¢する一考察 [Survey of current status of voluntary associations in the Tanba Area, Hyogo Prefecture], *Journal of the Japanese Institute of Landscape Architecture* 63(5): 709–714.
URL: `http://ci.nii.ac.jp/naid/110004305120/en/`

Fukuda, M. (1992). *Developing A Contextualized Church As A Bridge To Christianity in Japan*, PhD thesis, Pasadena: Fuller Theological Seminary.

Fukuda, M. (1993). 文脈化教会の形成 *[Forming contextualized churches]*, Tokyo: Harvest Time Ministries Publishing.

Fukuda, M. (2002). バルナバのように人を育つ *[Mentoring like Barnabas]*, Tokyo: Inochi no Kotoba.

Fukuda, M. (2005). Incarnational approaches to the Japanese people using house church strategies, *Sharing Jesus Effectively in the Buddhist World*, Pasadena, CA: William Carey Library.

Fukuda, M. (2010). 敬天愛人 *[Love God, Honour Neighbour]*, Tokyo: Jibikiami.

Fukushige, A. and Spicer, D. (2007). Leadership preferences in Japan: an exploratory study, *Leadership & Organization Development Journal* 28(6): 508–530.

Garrison, D. (1999). *Church Planting Movements*, Richmond, Virginia: International Mission Board of the Southern Baptist Convention.

Garrison, D. (2004). Church Planting Movements: The Next Wave, *International Journal of Frontier Missions* **21**.

Garrison, D. (2010). Leadership in church planting movements, http://www.churchplantingmovements.com/index.php?option=com_content&view=article&id=62:leadership-in-church-planting-movements&catid=39:leadership-dev-and-mult&Itemid=83, accessed 2010-05-21.

Gill, R. (2006). *Theory and Practice of Leadership*, Thousand Oaks, California: Sage Publications.

Goleman, D., Boyatzis, R. and McKee, A. (2003). *The New Leaders: Transforming the Art of Leadership into the Science of Results*, London: Warner Books.

Guthrie, D. (1990). *The Pastoral Epistles*, Leicester: Inter-Varsity Press.

Hayashi, F. and Matsubara, T. (1998). The influence of subordinate readiness on leadership effectiveness, *The Japanese Journal of Administrative Science* **12**(2): 103–112.

Hayashi, S. and Baldwin, F. (1988). *Culture and management in Japan*, Tokyo: Univ of Tokyo Press.

Hendry, J. (1998). The contribution of social anthropology to Japanese studies, *in* J. Hendry (ed.), *Interpreting Japanese Society*, 2nd edn, London and New York: Routledge, chapter 1, pp. 1–12.

Herangi, B. (2002). So, like, what's with these Xers, man?, *in* R. Tiplady (ed.), *Postmission*, Carlisle: Paternoster Press, chapter 1, pp. 2–13.

Hirokawa, R. (1982). Improving intra-organizational communication: A lesson from Japanese management, *Communication Quarterly* 30(1): 35–40.

Hofstede, G. (2005). *Cultures and organizations: Software of the mind*, London: McGraw-Hill Publishing Co.

Holt, A. (1995). The Moral Ecologist, *Third Way* pp. 16–19.

Hopkins, B. and Hedley, F. (2008). *Coaching for Missional Leadership: Growing and supporting pioneering in church planting and fresh expressions*, Sheffield: ACPI Books.

Imamura, A. E. (1993). *Urban Japanese housewives: at home and in the community*, Honolulu: University of Hawaii Press.

James, S. (2000). Dura-Europos, 'Pompeii of the Syrian Desert', http://www.le.ac.uk/ar/stj/dura/index.htm, accessed 2009-19-14.

Job, B. (2007). The Early Church Fathers and house churches: the subtle shift towards formalism (ad 100 - 300), *in* R. Zdero (ed.), *Nexus: The World House Church Movement Reader*, Pasadena, California: William Carey Library, chapter 16, pp. 173–181.

Johnstone, P., Mandryk, J. and Johnstone, R. (2001). *Operation World: 21st Century Edition*, Carlisle, Cumbria: Paternoster Press.

Kado, K. (2008). コミュニティを形作るものは何か？ 70-80年代の日本の社会学におけるコミュニティ論を手がか り に [What is community building? A guide to theories of community in Japanese sociology from 1970–1980], 2007旭川オープンカレッジ連続講座「あさひかわ学」報告集 *["Asahikawa-ology": lectures at Asahikawa Open College 2007]*, Asahikawa: Asahikawa National College of Technology, pp. 3–6.
URL: `http://202.252.170.6/research/staff/kado/com07.pdf`

Kawano, S. (2005). *Ritual practice in modern Japan: Ordering place, people, and action*, Honolulu: University of Hawaii Press.

Kawazoe, H. (2007). 非営利組織におけるリーダーシップ：類型的研究に関する一考察 [Leadership in Non-Profit Organisations: An Essay Concerning Typological Studies], 熊本大学社会文化研究 *[Kumamoto University studies in social and cultural sciences]* **5**: 77–94.
URL: `http://reposit.lib.kumamoto-u.ac.jp/handle/2298/3289`

Kobayashi, K. (2007). 地域社会のソーシャル・キャピタル生成におけるファンクルのポテンシャルを考察する [Studying the potential of social circles from the point of view of social capital development], 同志社政策科学研究 *[Doshisha University Policy Science Research]* **9**(1).
URL: `http://ci.nii.ac.jp/naid/110006404347`

Kotter, J. (1990). What leaders really do, *Harvard Business Review* **68**(3): 103–111.

Kotter, J. P. (1988). *The Leadership Factor*, New York: The Free Press.

Krupp, N. and Woodrum, J. (2007a). Church revitalization movements using house churches and small groups, *in* R. Zdero (ed.), *Nexus: The World House Church Movement Reader*, Pasadena, California: William Carey Library, chapter 18, pp. 194–220.

Krupp, N. and Woodrum, J. (2007b). The fall and rise of the Church: the principle of Restoration, *in* R. Zdero (ed.), *Nexus: The World House Church Movement Reader*, Pasadena, California: William Carey Library, chapter 15, pp. 167–172.

Lewin, K., Lippitt, R. and White, R. (1939). Patterns of aggressive behavior in experimentally created social climates, *Journal of Social Psychology* **10**: 271–299.

Lim, D. (2009). Church @ The Frontiers, *Starfish Files* pp. 3–6.

Malone, K. (2009). Doing evangelical theology with the Japanese, *Evangelical Missions Quarterly* **45**(2).

Marshall, I. H. and Towner, P. H. (1999). *A Critical and Exegetical Commentary on the Pastoral Epistles*, Edinburgh: T. & T. Clark.

Mathews, G. (2000). *Global Culture / Individual Identity*, London: Routledge.

Matsumoto, D. (2002). *The New Japan: Debunking Seven Cultural Stereotypes*, Boston, MA: Intercultural Press.

Maxwell, J. C. (1998). *The 21 Irrefutable Laws of Leadership: Follow Them and People Will Follow You*, Nashville, Tennessee: Thomas Nelson.

McGavran, D. A. and Wagner, C. P. (1990). *Understanding Church Growth*, Grand Rapids, Michigan: William B. Eerdmans Publishing Company.

Miller, D. (1999). *Reinventing American Protestantism: Christianity in the new millennium*, Berkeley and Los Angeles: University of California Press.

Misumi, J. (1964). The structure and function of leadership in education and industry: Proposed study, *The Annual report of educational psychology in Japan* 4: 83–106, 131.

Misumi, J. (1995). The development in Japan of the Performance-Maintenance (PM) theory of leadership, *Journal of Social Issues* 51: 213–228.

Morgan, G. (2006). *Images of Organization*, Thousand Oaks, California: Sage Publications.

Morgenthaler, S. (2007). Leadership in a flattened world: Grassroots culture and the demise of the CEO model, *in* D. Pagitt and T. Jones (eds), *An Emergent Manifesto of Hope*, Grand Rapids, Michigan: Baker Books, chapter 15, pp. 176–188.

Nacua, M. (2009). Field Report from the First Asian House Church Leaders Convention, *Starfish Files* p. 13.

Nakane, C. (1972). *Japanese society*, London: Pelican.

Niebuhr, H. R. (1975). *The Social Sources of Denominationalism*, New York: New American Library.

Oh, M. (2003). Study on appropriate leadership pattern for the Korean church in postmodern era, *Journal of Asian Mission* 5(1): 131–145.

Ōtsubo, M. (1990). ヴォランタリー・アソシエーションの発達社会学的分析：青年サークルにおける「余暇善用型の克服」をめぐって [Developmental-sociological analysis of voluntary associations: A case study of changing leisure orientations in a young people's circle], 弘前大学教育学部紀要 *[Journal of the Faculty of Education, Hirosaki University]* **64**: 83–100.
URL: `http://repository.ul.hirosaki-u.ac.jp/dspace/bitstream/10129/379/1/AN00211590_64_83.pdf`

Ōtsubo, M. (1998). 文化運動の普及に関する実証的研究 [Study on the spread of cultural movements], *Technical report*, Hirosaki University Department of Pedagogy.

Pew Forum (2009). Many Americans Mix Multiple Faiths, `http://pewforum.org/uploadedfiles/Topics/Beliefs_and_Practices/Other_Beliefs_and_Practices/multiplefaiths.pdf`, accessed 2010-05-21.

Pilling, E. (2010). *A critical evaluation of character formation in Christian leaders with reference to Jesus' character formation of the Twelve*, Master's thesis, Gloucester: Redcliffe College.

Pulley, M., McCarthy, J. and Taylor, S. (2000). E-leadership in the networked economy, *Leadership in Action* **20**(3): 1–7.

Ramseyer, R. L. (1995). Leadership and Church Organization in the Japanese Context, *in* R. Sawatsky and G. Hutton (eds), *Hayama Missionary Seminar*, Vol. 36, pp. 14–30.

Reid, J. (1980). *The house church, fad or model for future ministry?: a study of recent trends in the house church structure for Christian ministry and its implications for Southern Baptist Church development*, PhD thesis, San Francisco Theological Seminary.

Sanders, E. (1983). *Paul, the Law and the Jewish People*, London: SCM Press.

Schwarz, C. (1996). *Natural Church development: a guide to eight essential qualities of healthy Churches*, Saint Charles, IL: Churchsmart Resources.

Seki, F., Takaoka, S., Misumi, J. and Misumi, E. (1992). An empirical study of leadership development on the basis of PM leadership theory, *Memoirs of Kyushu University School of Health Sciences* **19**: 37–40.
URL: *http://ci.nii.ac.jp/naid/110000055167/en/*

Simson, W. (2001). *Houses that Change the World: The Return of the House Church*, Waynesboro, GA: OM Publishing.

Simson, W. (2007). The Five-Fold Ministry: God's Resource for Multiplying House Churches, *in* R. Zdero (ed.), *Nexus: The World House Church Movement Reader*, Pasadena, California: William Carey Library, chapter 50, pp. 430–438.

Smith, P., Misumi, J., Tayeb, M., Peterson, M. et al. (1989). On the generality of leadership style measures across cultures, *Journal of Occupational Psychology* **62**(2): 97–109.

Sullivan, L. H. (1896). The Tall Office Building Artistically Considered, *Lippincott's Magazine* .

Taka, I. and Foglia, W. (1994). Ethical aspects of "Japanese leadership style", *Journal of Business Ethics* **13**(2): 135–148.

Takahara, R. and Yamashita, M. (2004). 質問紙法による日本の産業場面における状況対応的リダーシップ・モデルの研究 [Questionnaire-based research on the Situational Leadership model in the Japanese enterprise], *Japanese Journal of Interpersonal and Social Psychology* (4): 41–29. URL: `http://ir.library.osaka-u.ac.jp/metadb/up/LIBJJISP/jjisp04_040.pdf`

Thach, E. (2002). The impact of executive coaching and 360 feedback on leadership effectiveness, *Leadership & Organization Development Journal* **23**(4): 205–214.

Tiplady, R. (2003). *World of Difference: Global Mission at the Pic 'n' Mix Counter*, Carlisle, Cumbria: Paternoster Press.

Turner, M. (1989). Ecclesiology in the Major 'Apostolic' Restorationist Churches in the United Kingdom, *Vox Evangelica* **19**: 83–108.

van Wolferen, K. (1990). *The enigma of Japanese power: people and politics in a stateless nation*, New York: Vintage Books.

Viola, F. (2008). *Reimagining Church*, Colorado Springs: David C. Cook.

Wagner, C. P. (1998a). The new apostolic reformation, *in* H. Caballeros and M. Winger (eds), *The Transforming Power of Revival*, Buenos Aires: Peniel Press, chapter 14.

Wagner, C. P. (ed.) (1998b). *The New Apostolic Churches*, Ventura: Gospel Light Publications.

Walker, A. (1998). *Restoring the kingdom: the radical Christianity of the House Church Movement*, 2nd edn, Westbury: Eagle.

Walker, A. (2002). Crossing the Restorationist Rubicon: From House Church to New Church, *Fundamentalism, Church and Society*, London: SPCK.

Weber, M., Roth, G. and Wittich, C. (1978). *Economy and society: An outline of interpretive sociology*, Berkeley and Los Angeles: University of California Press.

Wesley, J. (1860a). *The Works of the Rev. John Wesley: Volume I*, London: John Mason.

Wesley, J. (1860b). *The Works of the Rev. John Wesley: Volume VIII*, London: John Mason.

White, L. M. (1987). Social authority in the house church setting and Ephesians 4:1-16, *Restoration Quarterly* **29**(4): 209-228.

Witzel, M. (2007). The Leaders and the Led: Dyadic Approaches to Leadership, *in* J. Gosling, P. Case and M. Witzel (eds), *John Adair: Fundamentals of Leadership*, Basingstoke: Palgrave, chapter 4, pp. 55-72.

Wright, N. (1991). Restorationism and the house church movement, *Themelios* (16): 4-8.

Wright, N. (2003). Does revival quicken or deaden the church? a comparison of the 1904 Welsh Revival and John Wimber in the 1980s and 1990s, *in* A. Walker and K. Aune (eds), *On Revival*, Carlisle, Cumbria: Paternoster Press.

Wright, T. (2004). *Paul for Everyone: The Pastoral Letters: 1 and 2 Timothy and Titus*, London: SPCK.

BIBLIOGRAPHY

Yang, I. (2006). Jeong exchange and collective leadership in Korean organizations, *Asia Pacific Journal of Management* **23**(3): 283–298.

Yoshioka, R. (2006). *An empirical test of the Situational Leadership® model in Japan*, Master's thesis, The University of Texas at Arlington.

Zdero, R. (2007a). Apostolic Strategies for Growing and Connecting the Early House Churches, *in* R. Zdero (ed.), *Nexus: The World House Church Movement Reader*, Pasadena, California: William Carey Library, chapter 10, pp. 119–129.

Zdero, R. (2007b). Constantine's revolution (ad 300 and beyond), *in* R. Zdero (ed.), *Nexus: The World House Church Movement Reader*, Pasadena, California: William Carey Library, chapter 17, pp. 182–193.

Zdero, R. (2007c). *Nexus: The World House Church Movement Reader*, Pasadena, California: William Carey Library.

Appendix A

Survey questionnaire

First, some questions about your experience of house church.

まず最初に、あなた自信のハウスチャーチの経験について質問させてください。

How long have you been part of the house church movement in Japan?

どのくらい日本のハウスチャーチ運動に関わっていますか?

What is the name of your house church network? (If it has one)

あなたが所属しているハウスチャーチネットワーク名は何ですか? (もしあれば)

APPENDIX A. SURVEY QUESTIONNAIRE

When did your house church network start?

あなたのハウスチャーチネットワークはいつ始りましたか?

How many active meeting groups does your network consist of?

活動が盛んなグループ数はどのくらいですか?

Now, some questions about leadership in house churches.

次にハウスチャーチでのリーダーシップについて質問させてください。

Do you speak about "leaders" or "leadership" in your churches?

あなたのハウスチャーチでは「指導者」 または「リーダーシップ」などについて話したりしますか?

Do you have a defined "leader" when your church groups meet?

集会の際には、リーダーと任命された人がいますか?

If so, what does that person do, as leader?

もしそうなら、リーダーとしてどのような事をされていますか?

Are there other "leaders" within your network, and what do they do?
集会担当以外の「リーダー」が他にもいますか？　もしそうなら、彼らの役割は何ですか？

How are leaders chosen?
「リーダー」はどのように選ばれていますか？

What is required for someone to be a leader?
「リーダー」になる為には何が必要だと思いますか？

Do you use mentoring, coaching, or accountability relationships?
「メンターリング」、「コーチング」、「アカウンタビリティー関係」などを活用していますか？

Do you personally mentor new leaders?
あなた自身、新しいリーダーを指導していますか？

Do your network of churches use a leadership development programme?
あなたのネットワークにはリーダー育成プログラムがありますか？

Thank you very much for taking part in this survey.
ありがとうございました。

APPENDIX A. SURVEY QUESTIONNAIRE

Appendix B

Ten-Gai-Nai Cheat Sheet

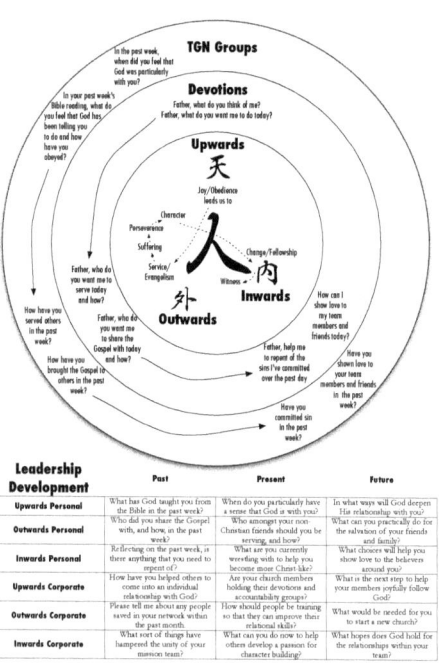

Leadership Development	Past	Present	Future
Upwards Personal	What has God taught you from the Bible in the past week?	When do you particularly have a sense that God is with you?	In what ways will God deepen His relationship with you?
Outwards Personal	Who did you share the Gospel with, and how, in the past week?	Who amongst your non Christian friends should you be serving, and how?	What can you practically do for the salvation of your friends and family?
Inwards Personal	Reflecting on the past week, is there anything that you need to repent of?	What are you currently wrestling with to help you become more Christ like?	What choices will help you show love to the believers around you?
Upwards Corporate	How have you helped others to come onto an individual relationship with God?	Are your church members holding their devotions and accountability groups?	What is the next step to help your members joyfully follow God?
Outwards Corporate	Please tell me about any people saved in your network within the past month.	How should people be training so that they can improve their relational skills?	What would be needed for you to start a new church?
Inwards Corporate	What sort of things have hampered the unity of your mission team?	What can you do now to help others develop a passion for character building?	What hopes does God hold for the relationships within your team?

Appendix C

Interviews

C.1 Initial interview with M - 2009-10-01

Worked as a church planter for 20 years, for the past 5 years part of house church network. Wonders why there are so few house church planters in East Japan; has heard estimates of 30 house church planters in Nishinomiya. Main influences are Frank Viola and David Watson. (Southern Baptist.) Has developed his own training system called 'ETA', a 6-session program. Has currently 20 people being trained. Aims are to evangelise through natural groups rather than pick out from isparate communities. Suggests I talk to YS from Campus Crusade.

C.2 Initial interview with G - 2009-10-29

Has been doing house church for 7-8 years; initially just with family, then with another missionary, then for the past two years with Japanese in S city, as part of a network house house churches out of Hope Chapel. Kamakura Hope Chapel dissolved into house churches—Yokotsuka & Yokohama. Partnership between Hope Chapel and Southern Baptists. 2008 first branch planted. Now four churches in network; one of which associated with SEND. Has heard estimates of a total of 100 house churches in Japan. (Due to Mitsuo Fukuda) IMB in Japan has a number of networks; one in Chiba, with 2-4 churches which has been going on for 6-7 years; two or more other networks advanced to the 6th generation within 4-5 years. Suggests I speak to Christian and Missionary Alliance, MUP and Mr. T. O.

One church does not use the word "leadership" but someone with obvious leadership gifting has emerged; however, that church is not reproducing. Another church has an intentional missionary leadership. Another church reconstituted its membership and has thus turned in on itself until 3 years passed when evangelism reappeared. Sees merits to both hands-off and hand-on missionary support. No clear leadership development strategy.

C.2. Initial interview with G - 2009-10-29

Mitsuo Fukuda was born in 1956 in Hyogo prefecture. In 1981 he was ordained as assistant pastor of the Lord Jesus Christ Church in Osaka, and from 1984 to 1988 studied for bachelor's, and then master's, degrees in theology at Kansai Gakuin University. In 1990 he studied at Fuller seminary as a Fulbright scholar, receiving Th.M.-Miss. and D.Miss. degrees within two years. In 1993, he worked as a church planter for the Japan Evangelical Churches, based in Nishinomiya[1].

While at Fuller, Fukuda's theological focus was on the development of Japanese churches contextualized to the Japanese culture—his Th.M.-Miss. thesis was entitled 'Christian shrines for Japan?' suggesting a fairly radical approach to church structure. His D.Miss. thesis (cited here as Fukuda, 1992) develops this theme, contrasting the Japanese, Hebrew and Western religious paradigms, and suggesting the need for a three-level church structure of one-to-one mentoring and evangelism, small groups which pray for non-believers —here we already see some of the intentionally evangelistic, 'Power Evangelism' style elements of Ten-Gai-Nai groups emerging in Fukuda's thought—and provide opportunity for fellowship and witness, and church services contextualised through various expressions of native religious elements.

In 2002, the think-tank founded by Fukuda underwent a transformation. 'Mentoring Like Barnabas' (Fukuda, 2002) continued the theme of one-to-one mentoring that appeared in the D.Miss. thesis, apparently influenced by Robert Logan at Fuller, but Fukuda appeared discouraged with contextualization efforts and began to work on a ground-up rethink of church planting.

[1] Biographical sketch translated from Fukuda 1993.

The major reason why we changed directions stemmed from a strong desire to see New Testament Christianity actualized in Japan. It was discouraging and exhausting to see such little fruit come out of our publications, lectures and conferences. We realized that churches where direct access to God is encouraged and that have a flat and personal relationship structure, rather than hierarchical structures, reflect the lives of people most contextually.

Both transportation and transplantation are based on the idea of the translation of a model whose starting point is, in the first place, a foreign idea, and which must then be interpreted and then introduced into the native soil. But a fresh incarnation emerges in the soil of a culture where the seed of God's words sprout. (Fukuda, 2005)

Appendix D

Church multiplication and Leadership development

Translation of a conversation between Hideo Ohashi and Mitsuo Fukuda on the theme of 'church-producing churches,' from http://homepage4.nifty.com/rac/031e/taidan01/t0101.html (Accessed 2009-10-13.)

Hideo Ohashi is a pastor representing the Christ Community in the Japanese Free Evangelical Churches. He is the director of JCGI Network, which supports church multiplication and ministry development and is a nationally-recognized speaker. He holds a doctorate in theology, and his books include 'The Church Growth Handbook', 'People who grow, and people who don't,' 'Living in the 21st Century

APPENDIX D. CHURCH MULTIPLICATION

—366 sermons,' 'Jabez: Blessing in the midst of pain' and 'Ministries to aid growth'.

Mitsuo Fukuda is representing the mission strategy think-tank 'Rediscovering Authentic Christianity Network.'

Discussion topic:

> We can see more and more the signs of revival about to occur in Japan. A spiritual 'thawing' is beginning, and there is a pressing need for growth and multiplication of churches that can be recipients for this harvest. How should leaders be thinking about church and what should they be doing to head towards effective mission in Japan? Let's hear both from the theory and the practice of these two men as they think about next generation church structures.

Mitsuo Fukuda: I recently wrote an article for the 'Evangelical Theology' journal (issue 38) entitled 'Starfish-style churches: A recommendation.' Many Japanese churches right now are sliding into a 'blockade mentality' marked by aging clergy, and I compared centrally-organized churches to a spider losing its head and seeing a breakdown of the whole body.

On the other hand, you have decentralized churches which are like a starfish. They don't have all their life force at the center, like a spider, and they don't have hierarchical authority structures, but the authority is distributed. Small groups are self-determining based on a direct relationship with God. As an example of current decentralized organisations, consider Skype versus NTT, or Wikipedia versus the Encyclopedia Britannica. If you cut a starfish in half, you get two starfish; in the same way, the Early Church grew as a direct result of persecution. The multiplication pattern of the Early Church after the persecution of Stephen is a perfect example of a decentralized organisation.

Hideo Ohashi: I don't think we've really seen an application of organisational theory to the Japanese church. Church form and ecclesiology has been debated a lot at the theological level, but the question of how it actually functions is an organisation-theoretical one. I think it's a totally new dimension to just looking at it from a doctrinal point of view. I doubt that there are many people who have noticed that and started to think about where the roots of the problems are. Probably only a very small number. There's an extremely strong tendency to put the problems down to 'spiritual' reasons such as a lack of prayer or adequate Bible teaching.

Mitsuo Fukuda: When we're talking about 'revival' we mean returning to a more dynamic expression of church, but in the case of Japan I can't find an era in history that I think we should be returning to. So there's an aspect in which we want to get back to the church of the New Testament, and see an animated dialogue between the Japanese context and the Biblical context.

Recently I went to the Okinawa aquarium. There was a shark there swimming with the other fish. Someone asked why it doesn't eat all the other fish, and we were told that the shark was always fed and satisfied. Food was silently dropped in from above, so it didn't need to go hunting. There was no need for it take risks, it was provided for nutritionally, the water temperature was just right, they even cleaned the tank regularly. But could that shark go back into the ocean? No, it couldn't... which is probably very fortunate for the shark!

Hideo Ohashi: The tank is just like the churches, right?

Mitsuo Fukuda: The biggest problem for the aquarium is that it wasn't breeding, and it wouldn't unless they developed a very sophisticated breeding programme. There's risks in the ocean; it has natural enemies and it has to make sure that it doesn't get eaten itself, but even so it breeds. It *needs* adventure. There's a joy and a strength in depending on God alone. Those who do that will reproduce. If you only think about gathering fish into an aquarium, then you might get full tanks but the fish in the oceans will die out.

Hideo Ohashi: Another problem is, just like you were saying about spider-style and starfish-style churches, what happens in your aquarium-shaped churches if the senior pastor or leader changes? I mean, that's going to happen someday. I don't know if the churches which are large now will be able to continue. Right from the New Testament up to today's churches, you have the issue of churches which give off light in their generation and are of great worth, but then shut down. But I think the question still remains of whether that's a good thing or not.

One pastor said this to me: "In Japanese churches you see a single pastor spending his life working hard to turn a church that used to be 100 strong into a 200-person or 300-person church. But when that pastor goes away, the church will fall back to its normal size." That's the sort of thing you see today. My wish is that we're not content with that. I want to see churches that continue to grow even when the pastor leaves. I think that we have an urgent need and a problem in Japan to structure our churches so that can happen. I think that your idea of starfish churches is one idea that responds to that wisely.

Mitsuo Fukuda: I used to concentrate my ministry on internal healing, and I've got plenty of stories of people who are much better off after healing, but I think you end up being dependent on the healer or on such-and-such a healing seminar. The reason I concentrated on healing is because I had a theology which said that if you were healed and received abundant grace from God, that would flow over into serving others. But I realized that a lot of people, even if they get healed, didn't go out to others.

Now as soon as someone gets saved, even if they are in a position where they need healing, I don't just deal with that, but I encourage them: "Because God is with you, be someone who serves others. Pass on the grace that you've received from God to your family or relatives or friends or those around you. That's your way from now on." Honouring God and loving their neighbour in their everyday lives. I call it 'honour God, love neighbour' living. If they go with that guidance, they can be healed in amazing ways. Just like how the scripture says "make the path for your feet level," if you walk a level path then you'll be healed. That's the kind of paradigm shift I've been led into.

Hideo Ohashi: As another way to put it, of course, there are people who need healing, but the reason that they want to be healed is because they want it for themselves. There's a lot of dangerous factors involved there. If you honestly believe that the healer is not some person with a special power but God Himself, and you live in a way that's obedient to Him, then God Himself will deal with it and one day you'll realise, "Oh, I've been healed. That's already done." That's what becomes a testimony. But if you want it for yourself, then next time you'll come with something else that you want for yourself. No matter how much you give people, they'll always come back wanting more.

Mitsuo Fukuda: We're like onions! You peel them and you peel them and they just keep coming...

Hideo Ohashi: Right! And another danger, of course, is that you need someone with a ministry of healing. That's the most dangerous thing, I think.

Mitsuo Fukuda: You end up getting stuck to one person. I think there's a way of thinking that says depending on one person is a step towards depending on God, but I think that in a lot of cases, depending on one person can be a hindrance to depending directly on God.

Hideo Ohashi: Right. That's the possible danger in a healing ministry. I think particularly Japanese people all have a tendency towards dependence. They end up being 'groupies' of that person. So they'd never go to a church if the pastor didn't have the gift of healing! They say "Oh, there's no healing at all in my church." That's unacceptable.

Mitsuo Fukuda: I'm currently working on the idea of 'imprinting' on someone within 48 hours of them being saved.

It's the idea that we follow the first thing that we see after we're born. If what they see straight away tempts them into dependency, then they'll become dependent. If they see a model of directly connecting with God, hearing His voice and putting it into practice in their everyday lives, they'll think "oh, so that's what we do." It's very slow to say to someone who's saved on a weekday "we'll teach you on Sunday." I try to lead people either the same day or the day after to begin to evangelise. Or something like "just as Christ came as a servant, go and serve your parents." I think that kind of direction, "go and serve," is essential.

Hideo Ohashi: Actually for church growth, the most important 'leaders' are those who are only just saved. But in most churches nobody really recognises them as 'leaders.'

Mitsuo Fukuda: There's a widespread view of 'leaders,' isn't there—they come out of Bible colleges, they do an apprenticeship period, they get experience as an associate minister. If you think that's what a leader is, then of course someone who's only just saved can't be a leader. But the Gaserene demoniac was told by Jesus to "go to your home and to your people and tell them what the Lord has done for you". Someone who was saved today can already witness to their experience of grace.

It's important to help them to be able to do that, because when three years go past it's too late—by the time three years pass, all of the people around them are Christians!—you're pulling them out of the context of evangelism. It's something that someone can do precisely because they're a new believer. If, when someone first believes, you skip over the right way to live and start teaching them right theology, they're going to find it difficult to put into practice.

Hideo Ohashi: There's one survey that says the average Christian life in Japan is about three and a half years.

Mitsuo Fukuda: Well, that's the same as Jesus' public ministry!

Hideo Ohashi: Someone said to me that if someone doesn't know six to eight people in the church to call them by name within the first three months, even if they make a confession of faith in that time, sooner or later they'll leave the church.

So we have to work towards building the kind of church where everyone knows everyone's names. The key is to build a community of faith. That's why I think that the multiplication of small groups, cell groups and house churches is very important as a spiritual way forward.

On the other hand, in a lot of cases, the idea of 'faith community' that a pastor sees is a faith community with the pastor at the summit, in other words, a spider-style faith community. So they intuitively fear that maybe small groups or cell groups are going to destroy the faith community. In 1977, I decided I was going to be a 'lay pastor supporter,' said "I'm leaving it to you guys" and took my hands off the wheel. And then in a meeting of Free Evangelical pastors, I said "This is how we have lay people pastoring churches. And they do the evangelism and the teaching. Oh, and they train others." and one of the old pastors gave the 'advice' that "if you do that, the church will split." So I decided not to bother talking about it there any more...And now, thirty years later, through good times and bad times, and we've had the church 'split' through multiplication, but we've never seen it split because of bad feeling.

Mitsuo Fukuda: One thing that's easy to misunderstand about organisational theory is that you think "we've got to stop doing it this way and start doing it another way" in a kind of radical break. It doesn't go that easily. So, start small, do what you can. Work out who is the first Peter or James or John that you're first going to pass the baton to, spend time with those people, share a vision with them, and give them the skills they need. Then just keep repeating that...

Hideo Ohashi: Just like Jesus did, spending time with those people is the most important thing, right?

Mitsuo Fukuda: For instance, for those brought up in the house church, they start by fellowshipping organically in families, so you don't need to break down the walls between laity and clergy; there's no walls there. On the other hand, if they've never seen a programme-centered church before, you have to teach them that that big building with the cross on it is actually a church.

Hideo Ohashi: The Brethren had a pattern from the start where they'd have no pastor or clergy but on a Sunday they'd share bread in someone's home and have no sermon but read the Bible together. I think that looking back historically, that's the closest model. The problem with qualifications and systems is that at the end you need to step back and say "well, how are we actually going to do that?" How do we get hold of

APPENDIX D. CHURCH MULTIPLICATION

it, or what do we need to change to get hold of it? Unless you think that through first, you're never going to make progress. I can say to my cell groups "take communion in your groups," but whether they do it or not depends on the choice of the people themselves. But a lot of pastors want to start from that standpoint—they end up coming in with thinking "is it right to let people do this themselves, or is it a bad idea?"

Mitsuo Fukuda: If we're going to profess the priesthood of all believers, we've got to start treating our believers like priests. If pastors only allow what goes on before their eyes, churches won't grow beyond a size that they can keep watch over, and the idea of filling the earth with disciples is a dead loss. It's whether or not they recognise that the Holy Spirit is in charge of everything, even things they can't see themselves. Jesus is with the house churches and cell groups, saying "fear not, little flock." If they aren't reading and interpreting the Bible for themselves, if they aren't hearing from Jesus themselves, then they will end up dependent on a leader.

To put it bluntly, the role of a pastor is a catalyst; so if people don't have an atmosphere where they can say about the pastor's ideas "well, that wouldn't work in my workplace," then they won't grow up to be independent. You won't get a decentralized-style organisation unless you have people learning from one another.

Hideo Ohashi: That's right. In a decentralized organisation, when one group divides into two, it doesn't mean anything if you just have one group and another group; you won't see a result until they're both about one-and-a-half times the size. A lot of churches have groups of ten people breaking into groups of five, but that doesn't change the total; that's not a result.

Mitsuo Fukuda: If someone slips and falls in deep snow and they just have their arm sticking out, someone who comes along afterwards can only help by pulling not just the arm but the whole body out. Ralph Neighbour, the author of 'Cell Church Handbook', talks about '*oikos* evangelism.' Because we're all in a network of human relationships, we can think about pulling out and saving the whole network of people. That's also the principle of church planting—we don't pull people who've been saved to where we are, we start new churches in the midst of the relationships that they're already in. We start churches with our neighbours, the kind of people we'd send Christmas cards to. So it's not a case of "if you get up to fifteen people, divide into two groups," but "if you get up to fifteen people, you need to repent of the fact that you haven't birthed a new church."

I used to pastor a church with a fairly traditional view of church, and it took a long, difficult time for me to turn it into a house church. Of course I had to change myself, and the people in the church had to change. If I changed too quickly, they'd all be saying "hang on a minute!" But if the average Christian life really is three and a half years, some people were going to leave the church anyway, so we trained up those young people and we were able to get on with a much faster pioneer planting sitation than we'd seen before. We had more and more dynamic people coming to faith through the witness of those who came to faith in these pioneer churches. We were able to plant churches on a new kind of foundation. The change got faster as we gave birth to deeper generations. There was a new DNA at work.

APPENDIX D. CHURCH MULTIPLICATION

Hideo Ohashi: The established churches are now starting to see a need for change, but even if they recognise that I think it's not clear to them how they need to change. Even if we put forward this idea of starfish-style cell or house churches I don't think many people would be able to accept it. So I think the change has to start with those believers who are on the forefront. If you propose in a kind of top-down fashion that this is how we're going to do church from now on, that's hardly a change from the top-down style that churches have been living in so far! I think there's a need for pastors and denominations to think and study a bit more about how they're going to start that process of change and what direction they want to head in.

The Japanese church always starts not from principles but by looking for a 'model church', getting in pastors from big churches overseas to give lectures so they can say 'ah, that's how we should do it,' and of course nine times out of ten it doesn't work!

Mitsuo Fukuda: Sure, but it's another file in the pastor's study...

Hideo Ohashi: And it's because they don't take the whole thing—the principles, not the model. It would be better if they have the understanding where they take the principles and say "OK, let's trust the believers with more of the work, I'll step down and if necessary become just another group member," and they follow that through, then it'll settle the question. And if they do that with the principles, it doesn't matter if the church they learnt the principles from is different to their own church. But no, instead they're just looking for another model of a big church to copy.

Mitsuo Fukuda: Even if a church has a lot of problems, if people are getting saved that settles it.

Hideo Ohashi: That's right. I think that's everything. To put it the other way around, the problem that's happening in our churches is that people aren't coming to be saved.

Mitsuo Fukuda: I think it's important for people to get fired up and excited about what God can do. In scuba diving, you have a practice pool, and you get thinking, "wow, is this how much I float? I want to try this in the ocean now," and then you go out into the ocean with an instructor, and it's a bit scary but you realise how enjoyable it is. In the same way, if you wait on the Holy Spirit you can evangelise even though it's a bit scary, and I think it's it good to have a structure where people can do that. When we train people we always get them out in a real life evangelisation scenario of the training...whether they like it or not!

When I ask pastors what's the happiest part of church, they tell me "being around when someone gets saved." I think it's unfair that only the pastors get to experience that joy. Shouldn't everyone experience it? If they start by catching hold of that passion for mission, then the techniques can come later.

Hideo Ohashi: I think we end up making evangelism difficult. With a hierarchy between pastors and laity, I don't think it needs to be said, but you end up with vertical relationships, you end up with walls between them, and people think that evangelism is something you do from behind the pulpit, when you bring in an evangelist to run a special evangelistic meeting, and people have done their work of evangelism by bringing their family or their friends along. And so this specialisation of evangelism between the laity and the evangelist means that evangelism becomes something that's reserved for a certain elite portion of the church.

I was saved as a high school student through the hi-ba movement, but I used to evangelise even before I was sure of my own faith! And so since I was brought up with that kind of experience I find evangelism fun; it's certainly not something that I feel forced into, or that I needed to do any special study to be able to evangelise. It's just that I have such joy and fire of being saved, I can't shut up about it! But so often in today's churches that becomes the specialisation of the evangelist. Believers are told that they need to evangelise but nobody tells them how to do it, so they think, well, there's an evangelistic meeting in autumn so I'll bring people to that. And when they look back, the believers will say, "I don't need to tell the Gospel to people myself. It would be awful if I told people something wrong anyway," and we raise up a load of Christians who can't evangelise.

Mitsuo Fukuda: I think church growth is not a matter of what technologies we use but it's believing in God and standing on His promises that "remain in me and you will bear fruit," or "if it dies, it produces many seeds" And it's a Biblical principle that we should "be fruitful and multiply, fill the earth" through generation giving birth to generation. The struggle is to set into motion that cycle where churches give birth to churches, disciples give birth to disciples.

Hideo Ohashi: That's right. I recently read the book "Between Animate and Inanimate" by Shinichi Fukuoka (a professor at Aoyama Gakuin University) and the subtitle of the book is "What is life?" He defines life as "a system for self-reproduction." It's easy to understand. I read that and I thought "the life of our churches is completely back-to-front." We might want to call it a "spiritual" life, but even in the Bible, life is about reproduction, and not just energy, strength or the ability to overcome difficulties.

Mitsuo Fukuda: It's like a coffee maker—if you put high quality coffee into a coffee maker, you might think that the coffee has 'life', but it's just a machine, it has no life. If it had life, it would be making more coffee makers!

Hideo Ohashi: I think it's the same with churches. If a church has life, it should be naturally producing more churches. If a Christian has life, he should be producing more Christians. I think that's a good way of thinking about life. God's purpose is to build His church, and so church multiplication is His will.

But if you think of church in this way, then having a traditional pastor or having elders or a church constitution... I think you have to put a distance between that and what it means to be a church. You've got to think that a different kind of church would be more appropriate.

Mitsuo Fukuda: In the natural world, multiplication is such an obvious thing that I think we shouldn't be saying "let's have church multiplication," but "let's put aside the obstacles to multiplication." That puts the focus on whatever is going on in our churches that is *un*-natural.

APPENDIX D. CHURCH MULTIPLICATION

Hideo Ohashi: That's right. I heard Dr. A. B. Seider from Dallas Theological Seminary say a while back that "in America, churches are getting smaller because big churches want to get bigger." We haven't realized that in the Japanese church, we're still aiming at how many people we can get to one meeting. That does have some possibility of expanding, but small groups giving birth to more small groups one after another, that would be great, I think.

The first issue is that reproduction isn't taking place, either at the church level or at the personal level. We're not putting out practical ways and means for that reproduction to be possible. Then there's the problem that pastors are so high and mighty that they're far removed from the coalface. Even a pastor in his prime gets pulled around by elders' meetings and interdenominational conferences. To put it another way, the churches are like teams with the ace away and the striker away. Unless we sort this out...there'll be no end of problems!

But even so, I still hold out hope for the future in the new kind of church movements that we haven't seen before. I've got the impression that there is a change coming. Young pastors under 45 are going to see that change happen. Generationally speaking, it's the Net generation, the change in the social environment that's influencing their thinking. Even fairly extreme thoughts are now getting more of an airing and a resonance to them. That's a bit more difficult when you're fifty. It's probably impossible when you're sixty! The Boomer generation see church growth as a kind of competitive principle, and if you end up seeing things with that kind of fixed ideas, it's the most difficult thing for church growth, I think.

Mitsuo Fukuda: Jesus saw the crowds 'bewildered and helpless, like sheep without a shepherd' and he had pity on them. I think unless you start from that heart of pity, it doesn't matter if you talk about 'church growth' or if you don't, from the point of view of the Kingdom of God, there wouldn't be any positive meaning to what you're doing.

D.1 Interactivity and Every Member Ministry

Mitsuo Fukuda: For about five years, I've not preached a sermon in my churches. I love writing sermons, and I think it's great to share what you've discovered about God, but I found that sermons weren't changing the way that people in the churches actually lived. They might increase knowledge, but they don't change lifestyle.

Hideo Ohashi: That's right.

Mitsuo Fukuda: So instead of preaching sermons, I've taken to doing 'interactive Bible studies.' The idea is that it's not a one-way teaching from the preacher, but all the members learn together from one another. I think there are probably people who have misgivings about the idea of a preacher being there but not saying anything, but when they get used to speaking out for themselves, everyone seems to come to life!

Hideo Ohashi: Right, the believers enjoy it too.

Mitsuo Fukuda: Yeah. They start to want to talk. Of course, you get problems when everyone starts talking at once, but...so we've made the rule that each person reads a verse, and when we comment on the verse we start with the person who read it.

One day one of the old members had the verse 'Jesus replied, "If you were blind, you would not be guilty of sin, but now because you claim that you can see, your guilt remains."' (John 9:41) And then he said, "I was a sinner. I thought that I could see, but actually I couldn't see anything." I was there, and I thought that God was speaking directly to this man and humbling him. Right after that day, that man's life completely changed. Nobody could have told this man "you are a sinner" or "confess your sin." Only Jesus could have said that. He was taught directly from the Bible. And his lifestyle changed.

If I'd have given a sermon, I'd feel great myself as the preacher, but peoples' lives wouldn't change. Instead, without a sermon, people depended on God himself and their lives changed. Which is better? Obviously I think the latter is better. If you do things interactively, you can learn from someone who's just become a Christian, or from a child. It's a wonderfully rich way of learning. You're not just always learning from one particular angle, but everyone shares the various ways that God has taught them. There's a dynamic in that kind of joint experience.

Hideo Ohashi: I always say that, if you look at it from an educationalist perspective, the efficiency and result of sermon teaching is about 5% of what gets said. But if it's not that deductive style, like a sermon, but something where people can share in participation by speaking for themselves and working out in an inductive way how to apply it themselves, the educational result is more like 70 or 80%. So pastors always choose the worst way to teach...and they think it's the best!

D.1. Interactivity and Every Member Ministry

Mitsuo Fukuda: People aren't very likely to put into practice what they hear from others, but there's a much higher probability that they'll do what they said for themselves. And if you move on from saying it to doing it, that truth really becomes your own thing.

Hideo Ohashi: That's right.

Mitsuo Fukuda: It's a shift from the classroom approach of a monologue to a more interactive, dialogue approach. The interactive approach where everyone has the opportunity to say something, makes it more likely that they'll be 'wise men who build their house upon the rock'—people who hear the word and do it. I think the church has got to try it. When the storm comes, I think those that are left will be 'those who hear the word and do it.' In other words, a small change in the church is very important.

Hideo Ohashi: It's a priesthood of all believers thing, right?

Mitsuo Fukuda: That's right. I think the traditional churches can become house churches, ...I think that rather than changing into house churches, they're going to take some of the more every-member-ministry components from the house church and pick and choose to form a kind of 'hybrid church.'

Hideo Ohashi: The current church style doesn't really do the whole priesthood of all believers thing; in the end, the pastor himself ends up being the single priest. I think that if they still talk about the priesthood of all believers, it's because the pastor and the members both have the understanding that selected members from the laity become elders or deacons.

And if you ask if people other than those have a priestly role, the job of understanding the priesthood of all believers gets thrown over to the laity and they say things like "well, so long as each person has the awareness of themselves as priests..." Tht's the reality at the moment. The real question is to what degree the believers actually face up to this. I don't think every believer does understand this correctly.

Mitsuo Fukuda: Yeah. Lots of believers would understand it like this: "I come along on Sunday morning to hear the pastor's sermon, and that gives me the spiritual food I need to survive the week." But hearing and obeying *God*'s voice is a Christian fundamental, not something you just you do a Sunday. That's 24 hours a day, 7 days a week. And a 'fellowship study' where there's the opportunity to hear and obey the voice of God isn't just something for a special place and a special programme, but I think it's a fundamental thing in our everyday lives.

Hideo Ohashi: That's right, that's exactly it. Recently a lot of churches are moving to a sort of cell group model, but I always say "the center is cell life." But I don't think most pastors understand that. They start up small groups in the midst of their churches and then they go out and say "our church has got cell groups" or "We've started doing cell church." But actually this kind of cell group just gets piled up onto another layer of church programmes, and the cell doesn't actually have any real life of its own. And so they carry on without really letting the Word intersect their daily lives, and there's still a dichotomy between church life and ordinary life. In other words, there's a lot of people living their Christian lives like a potted plant.

D.2 Leadership is catalysis

Mitsuo Fukuda: In the book about decentralized organisations, "The Starfish and the Spider" (Brafman and Beckstrom, 2006), they say that one of the characteristics of starfish-style organisations is that the leaders function as 'catalysts'.

From a Christian interpretation, we could say that leaders don't express their own vision but aim for the vision that God has for people, and are set up to sacrifice themselves to serve that vision. They deal with the ideas of how to empower people, how to give authority to them, setting up an environment of transferring knowledge to them, helping them towards their own independent functioning.

I think this sort of catalytic leadership is a universal issue for a lot of organisations.

Hideo Ohashi: Putting it the other way around, that's the bottleneck in a lot of churches today. This is my own theory, but the ultimate problem is one of authority transfer. We've put up our churches and handed them on and passed them down without actually dealing with this issue. While we don't have the same kind of hierarchy as in Catholic churches, we do as Protestants actually have something pretty close to that in our churches. Why I personally feel that is because I haven't graduated from seminary, I was always part of the laity. It's only because I'm part of the Free Evangelical movement that a believer was able to be recognised as clergy, and I think that's one of the great points about Free Evangelicals.

Mitsuo Fukuda: You weren't just a pastor, you were secretary of the pastors' conference!

Hideo Ohashi: That's right, even though there were other pastors who had come out of a seminary! So looking at it from that persective I can see things that pastors coming out of seminaries can't see. And I felt that when I came a pastor, there was this kind of wall between me and the seminary-trained pastors, this kind of gap that I can't overcome. It wasn't something visible and it wasn't something stipulated by the church organisation, but I felt that there was this undeniably real wall there.

Mitsuo Fukuda: I think that kind of sense of incongruity that you felt is a probably a problem of how much real friendship there is in our quite isolated church culture. Jesus went to be with a prostitute and spend time with her; on other occasions he ate with tax collectors. Jesus went out into the world, he got his hands dirty and he testified to the greatness of the Kingdom of God. But now the church wants to isolate itself from the world and won't go outside of its nice safe bubble. I think it's a massive problem when we think about how we're actually putting the Great Commission of 'go out and preach' into practice in everyday life.

Hideo Ohashi: We used to talk about 'ordinary believers.' We might not say that sort of thing any more but there is still quite a gap between the clergy and laity. I'm not talking about a sense of respect for the person, I'm talking about a whole difference in standpoint.

Mitsuo Fukuda: In the house church movement, it's more normal to have a flat relationship. So there's no real sense in which you need to get over that gap.

Hideo Ohashi: That's right. You can talk about a difference in roles, that's a less usual way of understanding it. Going back to what we were talking about before, you mentioned catalytic leadership, and one thing that supports that sort of leadership style is the idea of mentoring or coaching. I think pastors who want to turn those leaders around them into catalytic leaders are going to be looking to those kind fo techniques from now on.

Mitsuo Fukuda: Right, but I think that unless the pastor themself is undergoing mentoring, they're not going to see why it's important or what they need to do. It's difficult to do it if you haven't been through it yourself.

Hideo Ohashi: When you go through it, you get to notice 'oh, this is the sort of thing I need to do.' I think it can't just be theory. I think you can see Jesus's leadership style as a catalytic style, and within that, Jesus used mentoring and coaching—and strictly speaking there is a difference between them—as the situation demanded.

Mitsuo Fukuda: That's right.

Hideo Ohashi: So I think there's a bit more research needed on that. And I think we need to start incorporating it into the regular syllabus for pastors.

APPENDIX D. CHURCH MULTIPLICATION

Mitsuo Fukuda: Leadership development has three dimensions: knowing, being, and doing. For the knowing part, a classroom environment is best, but putting into practice the things that you know is actually different topic altogether. The 'teaching them to obey everything I have commanded you' part of the Great Commission won't be fulfilled just by knowledge alone.

To move that which you've studied into the realm of practice, it's indepensible to have a relationship of acceptance where you can talk about these things, grapple with good questions about them, and think about them and form judgements for yourself. You need to be able to practice again and again in a place where you'll be forgiven for making mistakes. And it helps you to grow if you can have 'faith adventures' where you're in an environment where you have to rely on God, and you're heart's pounding and you try to put into practice what you think He's leading you to do.

Having the knowledge is certainly a good thing, but the question is not "do you know it?" but "are you obeying it?" And actually it's not real knowledge if you don't put it into practice. The idea that 'if I teach a lot, the people I teach will go and do what I tell them' is actually a myth.

Hideo Ohashi: Well, is it a myth or is it an act of faith? But I think that's a problem that has its roots in the Japanese education system. What we call 'teaching' ought to be turning knowledge into practice, but knowledge often ends up progressing no further than knowledge. And that's going on in the churches as well.

Mitsuo Fukuda: Yeah, it's a wrong concept, isn't it?

D.3   Training disciples to evangelise

Mitsuo Fukuda: 2 Timothy 2:2 says "Entrust what you heard me say in the presence of many others as witnesses to faithful people who will be competent to teach others as well." We call this the 2-2-2 principle. Timothy teaches faithful people and the faithful people teach others. And since Timothy was discipled by Paul and Paul was discipled by Barnabas, you've got a chain of five generations of discipleship depicted in this verse. In that chain of bringing up 'disciples who will make disciples', the important question is not how many people get saved, but how many generations it will continue for. Actually, in a movement where this chain goes on until the 13th generation, it's reported that it has reached a million people.

Leading a big group is itself a fantastic work; but when a church becomes dependent for its operation on a single gifted leader or a mature personality, it's difficult for the next generation to carry that forward. If a church has a leader like that, nobody else can imitate them. So you might come out of a 'church growth seminar' and think 'right, I'm going to do it like that,' but sorry, that's not going to work.

The watchword is 'keep it simple.' The Bible is about 'ordinary people' (Acts 4:14) and the work of an extraordinary God. Of course, you need to be first filled with the Spirit, but once you have that, the actual teaching and practices that you need for a church are so simple that anyone can get hold of them. Jesus' teaching was a simple one for fishermen to understand.

I teach that the simplest way to understand the Christian life is 'honour God, love neighbour.' It's a favourite phrase from Takamori Saigou, who wasn't exactly a Christian, but... Or I use the three words 'Upwards', 'Outwards', 'Inwards': relationship with God, relationship with the world, relationship with yourself and your neighbours. The initial training of how you respond to God in each of those relationships takes about two minutes. With a simple plan like that, people only get confused if you talk for *too* long.

For instance, let's say someone's evangelising in a coffee shop and his friend comes to faith. He's practiced sharing these 'guidelines for obeying God' in two minutes, so he can then briefly cover the first part of Christian training by drawing a diagram with a ballpoint pen on the back of a napkin.

Hideo Ohashi: When I first came to Itami to do pioneer evangelism, my first plan was to do a kind of house church pattern. It already had a few churches, and it was the kind of place with very narrow roads that you can maybe just about get two cars down. No matter how many leaflets or church information sheets you give out, people didn't come along. But if we did it house to house, people passing on the Gospel and being saved in family relationships or through their friends, you don't need leaflets. So we started with the house church plan, and the style and contents are a bit different to what you're doing, but I can recognise what you're saying. For me the principle and fundamental way of thinking is the same. But now, since we've introduced the concept of cell groups to Japan, that sort of concept is now commonly called 'cells.' I myself talk about 'cell groups' to outsiders. But within our church we never talked about 'cells.' I call them 'packs.' I thought for a long time what would be the best thing to call them but we settled on 'packs.' Lots of things work in 'packs' as a unit.

D.3. Training disciples to evangelise

Mitsuo Fukuda: I'm often asked for advice from traditional denominations and churches, and I say two things. The first is to make small groups which meet regularly, confess sin, and encourage one another. Don't say 'let's introduce those to the believers', but I challenge them to start with the pastor himself. I think those who rise to the challenge will see blessing.

The other thing is, I get them to go out of the church and look around at people. Jesus saw the crowds and had mercy on them as they were like sheep without a shepherd. The Greek word is σπλαγχνίζομαι, and it refers to a deep mercy that comes from the bottom of your heart. I get them to feel that. Then they realise that growing a church from 100 people to 200 people doesn't satisfy it at all from the perspective of the Kingdom of God.

Hideo Ohashi: This might be a ... dangerous thing to say, but when I started doing pioneer evangelism, I saw that groups like the Jehovah's Witnesses were going out in groups of two, and actually one was a believer and the other not yet a believer. And like a stick of rock, it didn't matter when you cut them, you'd see the same style, the same invitations, everywhere you went, that was the technique that they'd set up. But we don't have that in Christianity.

Mitsuo Fukuda: No, we don't really.

Hideo Ohashi: We don't do it at all. I think that's amazing. We say that Jesus told his people just to evangelise, but how do we teach people to evangelise or give them the skills they need or coaching or models, there's nothing. I thought, you can't set up a church like this. So we get people in from here and there and listen to seminars and think let's do this, let's do that. And we end up thinking, well, we've worked harding doing this and that, so I don't want to think about anything new.

Mitsuo Fukuda: What we do is, train people to give their testimony in 90 seconds. Say what they were like before they were saved, what they're like after and include a Bible verse, then get into pairs and practice it. Everyone loves it! When the seminar's over, we go out into the streets and do it.

Hideo Ohashi: We do it in three minutes, but it's the same idea. Before you were saved, how you were saved, after you were saved, and a Bible verse. You say, this verse was key for me. Then you write it down and read it back until you can go out and speak without the notes.

Mitsuo Fukuda: If someone who's recently come to faith is operating from a DNA of evangelism, they'll be witnessing to the taxi driver within five minutes of being in a taxi. And they'll tell you that it's fun! They'll have a big smiling face. And going out and evangelising is God's work. It's not that if you say the right things well, people get saved. I've always been able to speak clearly, but it was when I was first saved that others got saved the most.

Hideo Ohashi: That's because now, people who are listening to you know that you're doing it for a job! If someone's an amateur who's just passing the time, that's got the ring of truth about it. That's what makes a good testimony.

D.4 Bringing 'have-not' churches back to life

Hideo Ohashi: Matthew 13:12 says "For whoever has will be given more, and will have an abundance. But whoever does not have, even what he has will be taken from him." I understand that verse to have an important meaning for the church in Japan right now. Various reports and surveys show that every year, the number of churches closing down due to the aging population is in double figures; at the same time, though, the church is growing at about the same rate. What's interesting about that is that the churches that are growing are branches planted by big churches. What that means is that to those who have is being given more, and those who have little, even that is being taken away from them. I just noticed this. In 2002, the UCCJ had 200 pastorless churches, and they say that in ten years time, there'll be 500. What they have is being taken away from them. But there are people being saved and going into the ministry. It's the big churches that are seeing this. I'm sure in general there are some churches which are 'winning' and others which are 'losing,' but I think this tendency in church growth is the same. So I think it's very important to turn 'have-not' churches into 'have' churches. How do we bring them back to life? Is someone asks me if I can actually do that, then, well, I don't have a magic bullet, but I can think of some things that are specific important points. I can say particularly that we're looking specifically for churches that are producing something new, I think those are the ones that are going well.

Mitsuo Fukuda: The goal is to fill the earth with disciples, to change society. It's 'for recognition of the LORD's sovereign majesty to fill the earth just as the waters fill up the sea.' (Hab 2:14) For that to happen, there are two approaches: first, a 'renovation' approach to help the growth of existing churches, and a 'construction' approach to build new houses on vacant lots. I don't think there's a choice between good or bad there, but it's a matter of calling.

Even if the church type is different, we're the same family of God. We're building on the common foundation of Jesus Christ. God loves and has high hopes for both styles. So we need to recognise the differences and bless each other, and serve each other.

There's much that the new kinds of church can learn from the established churches. It's important for us to know, as this movement expands, how God has walked with His people historically. For that, there's much that the established churches can say in terms of experience and accumulated wisdom. On the other hand, I think the established churches can look at the new types of church and feel a cultural gap between them, but I'd like them to appreciate that the wind of a new generation is blowing through them.

Hideo Ohashi: The real question is to what degree the established churches can accept that.

Mitsuo Fukuda: Looking back through history you can see three kinds of reaction from established churches. The first is persecution. The second is 'We do it our way, you do it your way.' Finally, there's the sort of reaction that says 'get yourselves together!' I think the new churches have to stand on the understanding that those three reactions are always going to happen, and reaction with humility to the older, established churches.

D.4. Bringing 'have-not' churches back to life

Hideo Ohashi: Well, if you think about it in terms of a bell curve, you're always going to have about 16% of people against you, so I think you have to just let them be!

But to bring about a change, you need the role of a sort of starter motor which starts the engine and brings about a positive work. If you just leave that to history or to the change of generations, you get individual churches doing their work in the world, which is fine, but if you think about the whole church as the body of Christ, we can't just coldly say 'well, that church doesn't have much so it's fine, what it does have will be taken from it.' I think you need something to happen to start the engine there. In the past we used to look to seminaries to produce that sort of person, but now I'm being told 'we can't really do that in seminary.' Unless our graduates have the opportunity for continuing education, we'll only see growth in the areas that they particularly care about. When I look out over the whole Christian world, I think that unless the Japanese church starts doing something about this, change is going to take an awful long time.

Mitsuo Fukuda: Unless the starter motor turns quickly, the engine won't start.

Hideo Ohashi: It won't turn! I think it's important that we consider this. Unless we get a handle on this as a pastoral concern, it'll only turn very slowly.

Mitsuo Fukuda: If you want absolutely everyone to get moving all of a sudden, even if you're very persuasive you won't start something new. I think you need to start with a small group of highly aware people who get started with what they can do, and that provides evidence that it can work.

APPENDIX D. CHURCH MULTIPLICATION

When I speak to a church pastor, I'll recommend that they continue with 95% of what they're currently doing, their current structures, but I challenge them to use 5% or just 1% of their time to try something new.

Then I challenge them to put together a pilot project. When you test an improved strain of rice, there's a huge risk if you plant whole fields full of it, so you start with an experiment on a little corner of a test field, and if you can confirm that that goes well, you start planting it in other fields. I think the key is to break it down into small steps, and have a long series of little demonstrations.

Hideo Ohashi: Now, I'm teaching the churches that make up the JCGI Network to start from that sort of thing. And the idea is that that leads on to church multiplication. In 2006, 6 churches whose pastors went through our training started up their own church planting network in the Chugoku region. So having tried that, I think that's the best style. If you get something, take it home, and say 'yes, let's do this,' it inevitably ends up being another idea that gathers dust on your bookshelf...

In the case of Japan, we've been doing our church development having taken on Western thought, traditions and culture...I don't want to say uncritically, but certainly wholesale. Our theology has been on built on the same principle. For Westerners there's certainly things that they can go back to, but for us, we don't have any where to go home in that sense. When we want to get back to the 'origins' of church, we have to go back to the Bible. That's a great thing, and starting from there may be a revival in the widest sense of the word, starting from the way we do church in Japan. But I

D.4. Bringing 'have-not' churches back to life

think it's important that we need to work on putting together a some kind of model or standard.

APPENDIX D. CHURCH MULTIPLICATION

Index of Citations

Anketell, 43, 63, 82, 89
Avolio and Bass, 63, 89
Banks, 48, 89
Barna, 83, 89
Barnett, 4, 89
Barr and Barr, 77, 89
Befu, 59, 89
Bestor, 63, 90
Blake and Mouton, 73, 90
Boff, 21, 90
Bosch, 21, 90
Bovet and Seed, 9, 90
Brafman and Beckstrom, 21, 79, 84, 90, 135
Braun, 82, 90
Bulley, 7, 90
Church Information Service, 31, 90
Cole, 3, 20, 48, 50, 80, 91
Cozens, 43, 74, 82, 91
Cray, 67, 91
Dale and Dale, 20, 48, 91
Doi, 63, 79, 87, 91
Eckhardt, 20, 91

Feddes, 6, 78, 91
Fee, 86, 91
Fowlkes, 16, 92
Fujimoto and Nakase, 65, 73, 92
Fukuda, 19, 37, 48, 49, 54–56, 74, 79, 85, 92, 113, 114
Fukushige and Spicer, 57, 69, 92
Garrison, 14–17, 92, 93
Gill, 30, 93
Goleman et al., 23, 93
Guthrie, 86, 93
Hayashi and Baldwin, 50, 93
Hayashi and Matsubara, 70, 93
Hendry, 59, 93
Herangi, 84, 94
Hirokawa, 59, 94
Hofstede, 43, 94
Holt, 83, 94
Hopkins and Hedley, 85, 94
Imamura, 64, 94

James, 6, 94
Job, 5, 94
Johnstone et al., 14, 94
Kado, 67, 84, 95
Kawano, 43, 95
Kawazoe, 71, 95
Kobayashi, 66, 79, 84, 95
Kotter, 30, 78, 96
Krupp and Woodrum, 4, 10, 96
Lewin et al., 72, 96
Lim, 55, 96
Malone, 51, 96
Marshall and Towner, 86, 96
Mathews, 51, 96
Matsumoto, 60, 97
Maxwell, 62, 97
McGavran and Wagner, 16, 97
Miller, 18, 97
Misumi, 72, 97
Morgan, 83, 97
Morgenthaler, 22, 97
Nacua, 35, 97
Nakane, 45, 58, 98
Niebuhr, 27, 87, 98
Oh, 58, 98
Pew Forum, 31, 98
Pilling, 56, 85, 98
Pulley et al., 30, 99
Ramseyer, 64, 99
Reid, 14, 99
Sanders, 5, 99
Schwarz, 21, 48, 99
Seki et al., 73, 99
Simson, 1, 3–5, 18, 23, 80, 99
Smith et al., 73, 100
Sullivan, 81, 100
Taka and Foglia, 61, 79, 84, 100
Takahara and Yamashita, 70, 100
Thach, 23, 100
Tiplady, 5, 8, 30, 51, 83, 100
Turner, 2, 3, 11, 14, 18, 19, 100
Viola, 3, 20, 101
Wagner, 18, 21, 101
Walker, 2, 4, 11, 13, 27, 101
Weber et al., 27, 101
Wesley, 8–10, 101
White, 7, 101
Witzel, 77, 102
Wright, 11, 13, 16, 86, 102
Yang, 58, 102
Yoshioka, 57, 70, 102
Zdero, 3, 4, 11, 18, 23, 102, 103
Ōtsubo, 67, 68, 84, 98
de Mente, 45, 91
van Wolferen, 74, 101

house church
    definition, 2

www.ingramcontent.com/pod-product-compliance
Lightning Source LLC
LaVergne TN
LVHW051123080426
835510LV00018B/2208